Encou
with the
Unknown

Colin Parsons is a writer and journalist, specializing in the Roman Republic and Early Empire. A former Duke of Edinburgh Award judge, and former codes and cyphers specialist in the RAF, the author is chiefly known as the country's foremost cryptic-crossword compiler. This work, which appears regularly in the Daily and Sunday Telegraph and the Scotsman, has led him to puzzles of a less explicable nature!

Encounters with the Unknown

True Accounts of Modern Paranormal Experiences

COLIN PARSONS

ROBERT HALE · LONDON

Robert Hale Limited
Clerkenwell House
Clerkenwell Green
London EC1R 0HT

ISBN 0-7090-4624-3

Photoset in Palatino by
Derek Doyle & Associates, Mold, Clwyd.
Printed in Great Britain by
St Edmundsbury Press Limited, Bury St Edmunds, Suffolk.
Bound by WBC Bookbinders Limited.

Contents

Foreword

Gavin Valentine

I am frequently asked to endorse books dealing with the subject of 'The Unexplained', and I usually say 'No'. We live in an age of rehash – rehashes of other people's books, and then rehashes of rehashes. If we're not careful, books about the supernatural are going to become like fifties crime series on TV: all this material has appeared before – only the names have been changed, to protect the author.

That was why I whoopeed when I was shown a draft of Colin Parsons' book. It's new stuff. Europe in general and the United Kingdom in particular are the home of psychic phenomena – and out of the gigantic bulk of unexplained and incomprehensible events. Colin has taken the trouble to assemble material that hasn't appeared before. I have seen his notes and documentation, and I can guarantee to the reader that this collection is going to stand as a major contribution to the literature of inexplicable events. Colin Parsons carries on where Charles Forte leaves off, and proves that the latter half of the twentieth century is just as remarkable to the Unseen and the Unknown as it is for its scientific onjumps.

I was born in Vermont in 1926. We had a big house, pretty much out in the wilds then, but not so cut off as to make us feel isolated from the big world outside. I spent a lot of time in its great gardens from the age of four or five upwards, and I used to wonder about the old man who sometimes came down to the stream and watched me fishing, or looked at me from the trees and smiled when he saw me going for a swim in the lake. Sometimes I saw him walking up or down the stairs indoors, so I guessed he was a pretty close friend of the family – but in my young days, children in New England still suffered from one annoying feature of Old England: they were supposed to be seen and not heard.

At last I summoned up the courage to ask my father who the old man was. Mother was there too, and I remember how they looked at one another with a 'he's found out at last' expression on their faces. At least, that's how I would put it to myself now. Then, I just thought they both looked a bit worried and surprised. After a pause for thought, my father told me that it was Uncle Zeb, who was a little feeble-minded but who would do me no harm. I was strictly told not to speak to the old man, in case it upset him, and that was the end of the matter – at least as far as I was concerned. A kid doesn't have much interest in relatives who don't bring him gifts – still less in those who aren't a hundred cents to the dollar. Uncle Zeb just didn't concern me any more, now that I knew who he was. I used to smile at him whenever I saw him, and he'd always smile back, but that was as far as it went.

It was three or four summers later that Great-Aunt Anne sent for me to spend a month at her place outside Richmond, Virginia. She was the senior of the family, a diehard Confederate, and I'd been told that she had one of the best collections of Robert E. Lee memorabilia in the whole of the United States. She must have been about ninety by then, and as far as she was concerned, Abraham Lincoln and his successors were the worst bit of bad luck the country had ever had – she doubted, sometimes, if we'd ever pull through 'losing' the Civil War, and her whole estate wouldn't have raised an eyebrow if it had been jerked back intact to 1850. Grand old house, horse and buggy (no auto!), Negro servants, and all her time given up to charitable works and good causes.

To me, I'm ashamed to admit, she was a pain. She lectured me most days on the virtues of the Confederacy, and there was nothing bad, from World War I to Al Capone, that Jeff Davis and succeeding Southern governments wouldn't have managed to avoid. After a fortnight, I was counting the days to the end of my visit.

Then, one sunny afternoon, she took me to show round one of the attics given over to Civil War junk that there just wasn't room for anywhere else. I saw Uncle Zeb – not for real but in a photograph.

He was dressed in the uniform of a Confederate officer. It was an old, brown photo, but there was no mistaking that face. Great-Aunt Anne then knocked me down by telling me that he had lived for a while – and then died – in my own home in Vermont. He was wounded at the battle of Shiloh, and they never managed to get all the shot out of him. So, when I had seen Uncle Zeb wandering around the grounds of my own place, coming and going on the stairs, he had been dead for more than sixty years. There was the same scar on the face of the man in the photo as on the face of the man I so often saw – a childhood wound, I learned later, that had nothing to do with the Civil War. There couldn't be any doubt that it was the same man.

Now I started counting the days for a different reason. I wasn't scared – I wanted to see him again.

And I often did. In the end, I know I would have spoken to him – how I wish I'd tried! – but I guess my promise to my parents was still pretty influential over me.

When I was drafted in 1944, I came home for a short leave from military academy just before going to Europe. Uncle Zeb came down the stairs when I was alone in the hall on my last morning, smiled at me and said: 'You'll be home, boy,' and then – for the first time I'd ever known it happen – just vanished in front of me. No one in the family has ever seen him again.

I don't know if Uncle Zeb had any real foreknowledge of what was going to happen to me, or if he was just saying some encouraging words to a boy off to the wars, but I did come home again, and as the years went by I developed a passion for more knowledge about the Uncle Zebs of this world (do I mean 'this world'?), and I felt more and more that I had had a rare and privileged series of encounters that it would be wrong to push aside.

Since then, I've never looked back. My researches have earned me a probably undeserved reputation – so many people seem to think that, just because I know so many of the questions and the mysteries, I must have the answers too. I don't. But I do know, from a very great deal of first-hand experience, that there is a Reality behind our reality.

I receive, on average, twenty letters a day from people who have problems they want explained, mysteries they want solved, or who just want to tell a story. It is a pity, as Colin says in this book, that we don't have an army of investigators to follow up so many fascinating leads. Most of my letters are from cranks (Colin tells me that his are too), but there is such a hard core of sensibly expressed, lucid information that is very frustrating not to be able to follow all of it up. As it is, I now get an experience worth recording about once a month; the rest I pass on to agencies which specialize in this aspect or that of the Unexplained, and hope that they may be able to take a deeper, or maybe long-term, interest.

I can afford to be selective now, and I confess that I often indulge myself to the extent of taking cases that look as if they might have a special interest to me myself, out of proportion to their importance in the amassing of provable fact. This is selfish, I know, but after more than forty years as a researcher I feel I can allow myself a few excursions into the Unknown which hold a fascination for me in particular, regardless of their intrinsic value as data. And it can happen, too, that this sometimes results in my finding out events of types new to me, which might otherwise have passed me by. I am in wholehearted agreement with Colin when he says that there is such a thing as a 'nose' for the unusual, and I will quote a brief but spectacular example to prove the point.

In 1977 I had on my desk two cases that specially interested me. One concerned events in Wyoming, and one in my home state of Vermont. Both of them looked likely to require a long study, and the Vermont affair seemed more likely to be fruitful. But my instinct told me that the Wyoming business might reveal something unique. The letter I had was cagey – which is unusual in itself – but it had enough in it to get me on the move. I went to a large Wyoming ranch to get the details, and here – very much condensed – is what I heard (and later saw).

Three years before, Mr X and his wife (I never give names) had thrown a party. One of the guests was a high-ranking policeman – which was fortunate for everybody there, or they might have found themselves in a worse mess than the one that befell them.

The other guests were friends from town. As a special treat, the family's little girl, aged six, had been allowed to stay up later than usual, and she started to hand round the drinks.

Before the party had been going for more than a few minutes, a roaring suddenly began in a corner of the room. At first it was no louder than a revving motor, but it rapidly increased until the whole company was turning to make a run for it. The rancher told me that his first thought was that some kind of electrical storm was blowing up, and the best place for everybody would be in the cellar.

Then, between them and the door, where appeared a vortex, beginning an inch or so off the floor and rising to a height of about six feet. Husband and wife agree that it was bluish-white and had the look of crystal. No one tried to get past it. Motioning everybody to the far end of the room, the chief fired half a dozen shots into its base. No result. By now, the noise was almost too loud to bear.

Suddenly the vortex began to move across the room towards the little girl – 'fast as a cat', as her father put it to me. It made a kind of stooping motion over her, and then she was clearly visible inside the thing, kicking and beating against the transparent wall. Her mother ran straight to it, grabbing to save her child. She was thrown back just as if she had touched a high-tension cable, and her party dress was badly scorched. Then the thing was gone – and the little girl.

Everyone in the room was almost crazy at what they had seen, and the mother was hysterical and needed to be heavily sedated. The guests (all of whom I visited shortly after my arrival at the ranch) dispersed as quickly as they decently could. Mr X told me that one fear high in his mind was that the thing – or another one – would come back and maybe take his wife, too. But hope won out over fear, and he stayed all night as she slept, hoping that his daughter would return, rather than taking his wife and servants away and leaving the house deserted.

Nothing happened. The kitchen staff had heard nothing of the whole affair until the guests had come out shouting onto the stairs after the vortex had disappeared. (Strangely enough, they hadn't even heard the chief's automatic. A 'supernatural noise' might well be inaudible outside the room it was intended for, but why didn't they hear the pistol-shots? The kitchen is within calling-distance of the room in which the party was held, but nobody out there heard a thing. I saw the bullet holes in the wall, so the chief's bullets had not been swallowed up by the thing – though he assured me that he had fired directly into it.)

In the weeks that followed, the young couple helped each other to put their nightmare experience behind them, but worse was to come. Early one summer evening in 1978, the roaring came again. In a moment, they saw the vortex in the centre of the room, and the little girl – plainly visible – kicking and struggling against its glassy sides. She was fighting as hard as ever, as though only an instant had gone by, instead of an interval of more than four years.

The rancher pushed his wife to one side and threw a coffee table at the thing. It just shattered like glass, and the strange twister disappeared at the same moment.

A week later, it appeared again. This time a maid was in the room, and she fainted with fright. The whole household had known that some mystery surrounded the child's sudden disappearance from the household, but it had been tacitly assumed that she had been taken somewhere, for some reason, by wholly normal and human agencies. But the maid had recognized her at once, and said so when she came to.

At this point, the reader may well be asking: in the light of these astonishing events, why isn't the world ringing with this story? Why isn't the mystery of 'The Little Girl in the Vortex' being as eagerly discussed as were the sinking of the *Titanic* or the dropping of the atomic bomb in their own times?

The answer is simple: the authorities won't touch it. They don't want to know about it, because official recognition of such an event would demand some response from them – and there just isn't one that they could give. You can easily imagine that the people at this Wyoming ranch have not kept these sightings to themselves. The ranch has upwards of twenty people working on it. They all know what the maid saw. A chief of police and many citizens had seen it, too. But nothing can be done, because there is no social or political machinery that is designed to cope with such an event. For example: a little girl has gone missing – why no inquest? Because there isn't a body – or rather, the only body that has been seen is a body that is clearly very much alive. Or why not a search? Well, where would you tell a search-party to start looking?

The chief has been told not to try anything official. Following garbled reports of the maid's tale of 'little girl kidnapped by whirlwind', a few pressman trickled over, but there was nothing to show them – and therefore nothing that they would print.

It has been said that the mind's eye has a sad tendency to see what it wants to see. True, but the official eye has a sadder habit still of refusing to see anything it would rather not find.

This is why books like this are so important.

The vortex has been seen on five more occasions – once by fifteen people at the same time, at another party. People don't go to parties at this ranch any more, and the witnesses to the original event were very reluctant to admit that they had seen anything peculiar at all.

It is in this way that astonishing events that could change our whole understanding of reality are simply swept under the carpet. In another generation, how many people will believe this ever took place? How many believe it now? Even those who saw it with their own eyes are busy trying to convince themselves that it never really happened at all!

I remained at the ranch for three months. The number of sightings, and the number of people who had been actual eye-witnesses – over forty, at the time of writing – made me stipulate that I remain on the premises, until I had either witnessed this thing myself or grown tired of waiting. I think they were glad to have someone from outside who treated them like sane human beings, and they agreed.

Then I saw it – in the early evening, the time it always came. I saw the vortex, heard the thunderous roar and very clearly saw a little girl struggling and apparently yelling inside. My cine-camera was on in a second, and my host took stills. Nothing shows but a blur which could be anything.

The questions this weird happening raises are too numerous to go into here, but one fact is particularly odd: clearly, time, as we understand it, does not operate with the vortex, or I would have seen a skeleton, not a living child. How long does she think she has been there? Her struggles are frantic, so to her it must seem as if no time at all, or at most a few seconds, has elapsed. Yet she had been there for four years when I tried to film her.

I've mentioned the press. One last word on that. You won't find this story in any newspaper – least of all, strangely, in the popular press. You are bound to have noticed what one writer has called 'the peculiarly defensive frivolity' with which the media always handle stories of flying saucers, ghosts, poltergeists etc.

That fact, on the bottom line, marks the significance of this type of book. It helps all people who genuinely want to know the truth about the universe – and it is the right sort of book. It has been carefully researched, and the material is of the first quality. Too many such volumes are mere masses of hearsay or unsupported anecdote. This author has been at considerable pains to get evidence that is supported by the testimony of at least two people, preferably more. Where only one is involved, his primary task has been to establish beyond doubt the authenticity and credibility of these persons as trustworthy sources.

The possibility of fraud or faulty observation always exists, and the true researcher must NEVER be swayed by romance or the desire to tell a good story. Colin Parsons and I and many others have experiences and information about the Unexplained which are tenable and true, and we must not be affected by any emotional considerations whatever.

If a man tells me that he has been alone at night by an old church and has seen the spirit of a monk, I am prepared to give him the benefit of the doubt; what I am NOT prepared to do is to offer such a tale to the public as 'evidence' of anything. There are far more uncertainties than certainties in the field of supernatural observation, and for that reason it is vital that the certainties be ruthlessly sorted from the unlikelies and even the 'probables'.

Scepticism for its own sake is as absurd as belief for its own sake. Rare indeed is the man who can steer the right course between the two.

Colin Parsons is one such man, and to those who are seeking solace, or scientific knowledge, or just that prickling of the skin that comes to those who explore the Unknown, this is a book that I thoroughly and wholeheartedly recommend.

Gavin Valentine, 1989

Introduction

A friend of mine was on the way to an urgent job when she witnessed a car crashing into a tree. She stopped but there was already a number of people on the scene, so she drove on to her appointment. The woman happened to be out, so she drove home again. Less than five minutes had elapsed, yet there was no sign of a wrecked car, no emergency services and no crowd. Curious, she stopped and found no damage to the tree.

What's the answer? I don't know, but the commonest one is 'she imagined it' – which is to say, she had a major hallucination. That answers the problem well enough, if people who have hallucinations can continue to drive cars safely. But the big problem with this oft-used 'explanation' is: do people in fact have hallucinations on a regular basis or even very occasionally? The answer from all the doctors I've spoken to is a resounding NO! Actually imagining you've seen something as complex as a road accident shows a serious disorder – drugs or drink or illness – but even then only in advanced cases of dependence, over-indulgence or long-term disease. I don't know what my friend saw. What I am trying to say is that there is lot that happens in this world that we just write off under some fashionable heading or other.

A classic case. I took some quite startling notes from a seance I attended (I am not a Spiritualist but a journalist) to a well-known scientist to ask his opinion. When I had shown fraud to be impossible, I received that other pat answer, 'telepathy'. My eminent friend was emphatic: in cases like that, the medium was a mind-reader. Any form of 'spirit' power was rubbish. It was a point of view, and one which might have held water (although it is valid in only about twenty-five per cent of the cases I have witnessed).

By chance, some months later, I was covering a lecture on brain-waves by this same man. At the end of a most interesting lecture, he asked for questions. One man asked why, if these rays were so powerful, one mind couldn't pick them up from another. He was blinded with science and virtually derided: 'What passes for mind-to-mind transmission is mostly auto-suggestion,' went on my pundit. 'You may take it from me that telepathy is bosh.' This illustrates the attitude to psychic phenomena of many scientists. Rather than face something not scientifically demonstrable in a test-tube, they will downgrade it to a lesser problem, but they don't believe in that either, so it is simply blowing a raspberry at all new ideas and dressing it up in scientific mumbo-jumbo. There is nothing either surprising or novel in this: it's been going on for centuries. I can recall as a child in the mid-1950s reading a headline 'Famous scientist says space-travel is impossible.' You had to know the name of the man to realize that he was a biologist who had done his finest work in 1910 – he knew less about space travel than I did. And so it goes on.

The most important effects of this attitude are 1) the elevation of scientists to the old position held by priests – they interpret everything in the world by direct knowledge from God; 2) the public are taught to despise any new advances unless they receive the stamp of authenticity from Science, and 3) the public are made to feel that their experiences are trivial and based on 'hallucinations' and 'old wives' tales' and, as a consequence, they don't tell anybody about them. I defy any reader of this book NOT to be able to remember at least two incidents in his or her life that have left a lingering doubt as to whether it was a meeting with what this book classes as 'the Unknown'.

I am the first to bow to the achievements of science. It has set men free from gross labour, fears of disease and many of the horrors that were part and parcel of all previous generations' day-to-day lives. It must not, however, be allowed to live on the interest from this justly earned capital and retard the progress of new sciences out to explore things once undreamt-of. Some will turn out to be mares' nests and will o' the wisp, but others will remain and grow.

In writing this book I have attempted to be just to all. Many stories have been rejected for many reasons, and all in the interests of a fair and unbiased narrative. I have tried to balance the chapters to give a hearing to all those strange things on whose fringes we still are. Except in special cases, names and locales have been changed, but no fact has been interpreted, let alone changed, to suit my own prejudices.

I should be grateful to hear from readers who think they have interesting or useful experiences to relate. I hope that people will allow me to continue producing such books for as long as there are new tales to tell, and the public pays me the compliment of remaining interested in my collections of Man's encounters with the Unknown. No reader need fear that confidence will be breached. As with those who have entrusted me with their stories in this volume, all may count on my guarantee of absolute anonymity under any circumstances, and this is further supported by my membership of the National Union of Journalists, which commits me to keep secret the sources of any information entrusted to me.

For readers who are interested in the background to these reports, they have *all* been the result of face-to-face interviews with those who have had the experiences. There are not stories taken from third parties, other books or items published in newspapers, and it is the first time any of these accounts has been published, in whatever form.

My own interest in the subject comes from investigating and examining psychic phenomena in the mid–1960s, and becoming more and more convinced that this seemingly ordered world is to a large extent a mask for much that is both sinister and hopeful.

The collection, amazing as it is, is largely the result of hard work and determination on my part, plus other people's sense of duty. This is a point I should particularly like to stress: there is a whole world of strange experiences waiting to be investigated, but genuine people do not rush to journalists with their stories – quite the reverse – and those who have encountered the Unknown must be sought out and persuaded that there is a greater good to be served by candour than by reticence.

Over the years, I have examined thousands of those tantalizing snippets in papers that we all wonder at for a few minutes, then forget. Then I have gently approached the victims (and I use the word carefully) and attempted to show them that their silence is only making things worse for others like themselves (some who have been made very ill by brooding and fears) because of the ridicule that is heaped on such people. Those who have had encounters with ghosts, UFOs and the paranormal generally are very like people who have been raped or attacked – their instincts are to try to forget, and to limit the damage done to their worlds. But they do want to talk to somebody, to know that at least one person believes them, and to be told that they are not alone. Finally, when the trauma is eased, I ask permission to repeat their stories under a cloak of absolute anonymity. Many refuse point-blank, some contact me later with a change of heart, and some are only too happy to give others the benefit of knowing that they are not alone and that there are kindred spirits who have suffered all that they are suffering.

For me, it has been a slow but far from painful quest, and no reader should under-estimate the courage shown by those whose stories appear in this book. People who have experiences such as these are often deeply afraid; some of madness, others of retaliation from the things they have seen, but all are afraid of the scorn and contempt of their fellows.

As to my method of establishing the truth (I have printed reports mainly where two or more people are involved), I have questioned the subjects separately and together, and examined any physical evidence that remains. Other witnesses have been questioned at length, and all testimony has been carefully sifted. Any policeman or journalist will tell you that only a rare handful of people can deceive, unless the questioner himself is determined to be deceived. The only liar who has a chance is the solitary obsessive who has come to believe his own fabrications, and two or more people cannot maintain a deception in the face of professional questioning. There is, however, a more fundamental point: why should anyone want to lie? They have not come to me, I have sought them out, and the question of money or fame has not entered the proceedings. In my own opinion, these reports represent the unvarnished truth.

Anyone who reads this book and chooses to escape reality by ascribing conscious or unconscious fraud as a solution to the mysteries exposed, is suffering from a neurosis. They are making prejudice superior to evidence, and that is the negation of all the human intellect stands for.

Colin Parsons, 1989

HELPFUL GHOSTS

Helpers from Beyond

There are many inexplicable events connected with rescues, and there seems to be a large collection of spirits whose job it is to come back and help in times of crisis or emergency. Many of these are quite well-known, while others remain what might be called a family secret.

One of the more astonishing of these strange helpers is 'Old Bob', as he is affectionately known to a large section of the men who drive Eastern Region trains. When you consider that the latest report I have had on him was for 1983, although he was spoken of before the turn of the century, you will see that he is one of the most consistent spectres on record.

Old Bob simply appears on the track with a red flag by day, or a lamp by night, and brings a train to a halt, leaving it to his earthly counterparts to discover the nature of the danger. On a number of occasions trains have been unable to stop in time and have 'hit' him, but this has had no effect. He doesn't take offence and will turn up the next time he is needed.

Quite recently a driver new to the Eastern Region section, and to Old Bob, was taking his train through a narrow cutting when the figure appeared with his flag and the driver applied the brakes. The cutting had two almost sheer walls, and the line stretched clearly visible for a hundred yards or more. Furthermore it was a bright afternoon, yet in the seconds it took the driver to take his eyes off the figure and jump down from the cab, it had disappeared. Baffled, he inched the train forward to the bend, only to find sleepers laid across the track by vandals. The timely appearance of the warning figure had probably prevented a very serious accident.

Who Old Bob is remains surrounded in mystery. He wears the clothes of a man from the Victorian age and is dressed more as a porter than a driver, although no experts on old railway uniforms have had the opportunity to see him. Legend has it that he was killed trying to save a lady who had fallen onto the line, but that is the sort of romance that gathers about such sightings and is definitely not to be relied upon. There is no way of telling how many times he has appeared, because not every incident is reported, let alone given to a central monitoring station, but twenty or thirty times since the last war would seem to be a conservative estimate. He is quite unprejudiced and will save diesel engines just as he once saved steam. One strange thing about him is that many drivers have reported seeing a small red flash as their trains struck the spirit.

Also odd is the fact that after these accidents there is never a trace of the lamp or the flag to be found, and certainly no body.

Old Bob is one of those ghosts that attract scant attention and have simply become a part of Britain's great haunting heritage. I have heard of similar men in France and the USA, but I cannot vouch for these as I have never spoken to anyone who has actually seen them.

If Old Bob is a public ghost, as it were, Sister Angela is a very private one. She has her habitation in a small cottage hospital in the Home Counties. At times of emergency (as in a recent train accident) she is there as usual, offering aid and comfort to the victims and leaving the hard-pressed staff to get on with more important jobs. All new staff at the hospital are carefully instructed as to the nature of Sister Angela, and the proper way to behave when she puts in an appearance. She must on no account be questioned, and the most she has said in reply to anything is, 'I'm Sister Angela.' She then smiles and gets on with whatever it is she is doing. Patients who are not in on the secret always speak highly of the wonderfully calming influence she has had on them. Her uniform is quite modern, but no one has been able to identify it as belonging to any special nursing service.

A very similar sort of person is the clergyman who works his 'parish' in some of the more run-down parts of London. He is able to seek out those who are close to breaking-point and suicide, and many report having received great help from his kindly words and sound advice. He gives no information about himself at all, and we only know that he is of spirit and not body by the consistent evidence of those he has helped that he simply fades gently from view when he has completed his mission. The only thing we do know for certain about him is that he does good, and I don't think there is really much more to be said than that.

There is a similar story from further north, and it concerns a Catholic priest with responsibilities for a very large parish. In 1976, he had been sent for to administer the last rites, but appalling weather made it impossible for him to reach the house in time. When he did arrive, he was told that a colleague had managed to get there and that all the proper formalities has been dealt with. Mystified, since there was not another priest in the area, least of all one who would know that his services were required, he closely questioned the family and found that the service had been conducted most correctly, the priest then simply leaving the house in full vestments, despite the storm. No one had heard a car start, but as the wind was very loud, that is not evidential. What did make it more curious was that an almost exact repetition took place two years later, the priest in question answering the description of the man who had conducted the service two years before. There have been no further reports (to my knowledge) since 1978.

It does seem as if the spirit of someone who has recently died can be very effective for a short time, as we shall see in the case of the pilot who saved the aircraft in An Odd Miscellany I, and this case is similarly revealing. During the fifties a small coastal fishing vessel found itself in dire straits when its engine failed off some very hazardous rocks. A strong wind was blowing them inexorably towards their deaths when the figure of their friend Jock Robson was seen striding down the deck. So normal did he look that this strange sight did not excite fear – it was just taken for granted that he had been aboard for some reason. He went down into the engine-room and, as befitted the best engineer in the business, the ship was soon sailing away from the rocks under full steam. They waited for him to come back up, and when he didn't, they went down to investigate. There was no one there. When they got back to port, they heard that he had died suddenly at about the moment he was seen on board.

Such reports are very common, and I have used only those for which there were many witnesses. Whatever the true nature of death and the world to come, I think we can be fairly certain it is not the total annihilation some people think.

An Ancient Mariner to the Rescue

Of all places on earth, there can be nowhere that has a larger crop of uncanny events than the sea. Men of all nations and all ages recount strange happenings, but most are no more than travellers' tales, imagination under stress and honest mistakes. The Phoenecians used to tell terrible stories of the seas beyond Greece, with the very sensible motive of stopping others following their profitable trade routes. From them we probably get the stories of the clashing rocks and the sirens. Others told tales seemingly equally preposterous, yet containing truths we have only recently understood. Ancient sailors talked of the days and nights each being six months long and the water changing into rock 'at the top of the world' – and were laughed at; now we know they went so far north as to reach the Arctic Circle. Generally, however, all they saw were natural phenomena not known to their time.

In modern times, the stories are more in tune with the beliefs of our age: strange electromagnetic effects, UFOs etc and the Bermuda Triangle. This is not a debunking book, and I know of no reason to disbelieve some of the stories told about such places. What I do know is that the evidence presented does not come up to the criteria I have established for these reports.

Eric and Peter's story is a fantastic one and, were it not for internal evidence that proves it to be true, I should dismiss it along with mermaids and the Flying Dutchman, and other tall tales.

Eric and Peter were just out of National Service in the mid 1950s and were finding Civvy Street very boring indeed. They had only been ordinary soldiers but they had had a whale of a time, and long, tedious factory shifts were driving them mad. Then they had a brainwave: as they were both addicted to wine, women and song, why didn't they work on board ships, go to all the exotic places they had always dreamed about, have a terrific fling, then sail on to the next fleshpot? This they embarked upon without further delay, finding the life even better than they had expected. Work was rarely hard, the crews were friendly and the landfalls at such places as Port Said and Bangkok were exciting beyond their wildest hopes.

At a small harbour near San Francisco, on the west coast of the USA, they found themselves broke and without one of the big ships they were used to. They then had what seemed a stroke of luck by falling in with a group of Americans who jointly owned a small tramp steamer and who transported anything if the pay was good. Two members of the normal complement were unable to make this trip, and the captain was looking for two good workers who would come cheap and not query the cargo. There was nothing illegal in the business, but what was carried was sometimes very dangerous, which made ordinary hands a little wary. The two British seamen, however, saw the trip only as a godsend. An added bonus was that they would end up in the Philippines, a place they both longed to visit. Formalities were adroitly avoided, and the boat soon set sail.

They were about five days out when they were awakened by the call for all hands. Stumbling up to the deck, to their horror they found the ship on fire. Always before they had been on large vessels which were adequately manned; this short-handed cockleshell, ablaze on the world's largest and loneliest ocean, filled them with dread. With the characteristic generosity of their race, the Americans pushed lifebelts over their heads and hurled them kindly, but unceremoniously, into the sea. They instinctively began to swim away from the ship – for how long they have no idea before the night became a blaze of light and sound as the ship exploded. For a few minutes the wreckage blazed, then there was silence. It was at that moment, Peter recalls, that he gave himself and his companion up for lost. The dimensions of this ocean were so great that it was as if they were in John o' Groats with the nearest human being at Land's End, ignorant of their predicament.

Rain came with the dawn, and the rosy picture of the warm Pacific bathed in sunshine was far from the truth. They were very cold, very thirsty, very hungry and very frightened, and their chances of being found could be calculated in billions, not millions, to one. Too tired and dispirited to swim, they just floated as the light began to intensify, wondering what it would be like to drown.

Peter says he thought he heard a sound but dismissed it as imagination. Then it came again, the unmistakable plashing of oars. Someone rowing a small boat pulled them aboard, and they lay gasping in its tiny confines. As their breath came back, they studied their rescuer. He was a very big man, wearing a navy-blue sweater and dark trousers, and he was looking back at them with equal interest. He introduced himself as 'Ross', and his accent was broad Scots. His own ship, he said, had foundered in a storm and he had been rowing ever since.

They thanked him for his timely intervention and asked him how he had survived, there being nothing to eat or drink visible in the boat. He answered somewhat cryptically that 'there were ways'. This he proceeded to show by dexterously catching fish with his hands. To their surprise, he threw them all back, and they became increasingly irritated as, now they were safe, the intensity of their hunger and thirst had returned. Eventually Ross caught a big fish and grunted with satisfaction. Pulling it in half, he shared it out, instructing them to suck the water from it. They did and found a copious amount. They chewed on the flesh and felt much refreshed. They asked Ross about his own ship, but he seemed to become confused, according to Eric's memory, embarrassed according to Peter's. He caught two more of the fish during the day and was taciturn except for odd bouts of muttered talk, not seeming to be meant for them. 'I was a fool, they should never have died,' was said a dozen times, and 'Millie shall have it,' again and again. Grateful to their rescuer and sensitive for his feelings, he having been recently shipwrecked too, they refrained from questioning him.

As night drew on, they sighted a tiny island. It was a true desert island, having no natural water, but a large amount of rain had collected in hollows of the rocks. The vegetation was sparse, and life seemed extinct on the place, although they did hear rustling during the evening. More fish were collected (they knew so little of man that they could be scooped up with no difficulty); a fire was lit and they were able to have a hot meal and plenty of fresh rainwater to drink. Ross seemed to eat nothing, but once again they put it down to anxiety or grief. In the morning he announced that he was going, without saying where or why. Before he left, he asked them to do something for him, to which they readily agreed. He dictated an address and a number, informing them that the first was his wife's home, the second a safety-deposit box. The key was to be found in a hole in a ventilation brick in his shed, and she was to have all the box contained. The finality of these arrangements alarmed them considerably. 'What about us?' they asked. He assured them that they would be picked up within forty-eight hours at the latest. The relative security of the island, compared to the provision-less boat, convinced them to trust one who had so far shown them nothing but kindness. He rowed away, and they prepared to wait for him to keep his word.

In a very short time an aircraft of the US Coastguard flew over, dropping emergency rations and a message that a ship was on its way. By morning a big vessel had anchored off the tiny speck of rock, and a boat had been sent to pick them up. It took them back to San Francisco, where they were required to tell the harbour authorities their story. They told them of Ross, as they were anxious to know that he was all right.

The coastguard captain shrugged: 'All we know is that some guy hailed a coaster and told them to radio us with your position. As far as I know, he just rowed off again. It's our job to rescue people in trouble, not question people on the high seas. Thank your lucky stars; there are some guys in these parts who would slit your throats for the price of your watches.'

When Eric and Peter got back to Britain, they were as good as their word. A Mrs Millicent Ross did live at the address, and she appreciated the information about the box. When she asked how they knew about it and they told her, she almost had hysterics. Her husband had been dead for over eight years – he had been lost overboard from a cargo ship in the Pacific. How the large sum in the deposit box had been acquired is best not gone into too deeply, nor the question of what Mr Ross had intended to do with the money. Since the cash stifled Mrs Ross's grief and her curiosity, it may well be that Ross had decided not to return to so 'loving' a wife.

It was not difficult for me to go into the whole thing in more detail, and what I found makes this a truly astonishing tale. The Captain's log for the appropriate date in 1948, when the accident occurred, reads (I paraphrase the formal and nautical language): 'At 3 p.m. the wind which had blown strongly all day freshened to almost storm force. All hands were ordered on deck as a precaution and AB Ross was reported as drunk. A small fight broke out between the officer of the watch and Ross when he tried to launch one of the ship's boats, apparently under the impression that a hurricane was imminent. The officer was incapacitated by Ross and I ordered two seamen to restrain him. The boat and the three men fell into the sea and the ship stopped. All three were brought back dead and, in accordance with my duties, they were given burial at sea.' Very significantly, it is recorded in a subsequent entry that the ship's boat was never recovered.

Doctor in the House

In the early eighties, Mr and Mrs O'Rourke and their family might have represented those wretched people who are so often mentioned but so rarely met – 'There's always somebody worse off than yourself!'

Mrs O'Rourke lived with the three youngest children in a council refuge (the other six were in care), and Mr O'Rourke existed in a hostel for single men and spent his days in a gruelling and futile search for work. Without exception, the whole family were in poor health, both physical and mental, and the various agencies charged with their succour were at their wits' end to know what to do with them. Theirs was a story typical of people on the downward spiral. Having come over to Britain from Ireland in the late sixties, Mr O'Rourke had lost his job in 1975 through an industrial accident for which he received no compensation. The family lost their rented accommodation soon after and gradually drifted from bed-and-breakfast rooms to this final extremity of want and privation. Mr O'Rourke was no slacker – he did spend a great deal of time attempting to find something to do, but his injury had given him a limp, his clothes were threadbare remnants of their Oxfam glory, and he spoke with such a pronounced brogue that people found it difficult to hold a conversation with him.

As with most Irish people, however, the love of learning burned with a steady flame in Mr O'Rourke's breast, and when he was not searching for work he spent every available minute in the public libraries. He had natural facility for learning, and he was as staunchly catholic in his reading as he was Catholic in his religion. Privation did not have the effect of lowering his moral standards, a phenomenon that is one of the worst effects of unemployment. From time to time he was given odd jobs – shifting rubbish or mowing a lawn, and he always scrupulously gave a full reckoning to the Social Security office, much to those people's shame and embarrassment, for they had to dock this honest man's dole money while knowing that other claimants were working but still taking the full amount. In the spring of 1981, as though by action of a benign Providence seeking to reward a luckless but honest son, a house became available that the council considered ideal for the solution of one of their most intractable cases. A long-term benefactor of the council died, leaving a large, rambling house for them to dispose of to some deserving family. It was in the depths of Essex, in a comparatively large but remote village, and enjoyed ample living room for such a large family, together with the healthy country environment that it was thought would do wonders for their health.

The O'Rourkes, of course, could scarcely believe their good fortune. The council supplemented the furnishings left by the previous owner with enough bedding for the entire family, and various charities who had been impressed by their dogged cheerfulness in their adversity provided such luxuries as a TV and a fridge. The house comprised four truly gigantic bedrooms, a vast kitchen with an old-fashioned gas stove, two reception rooms, a couple of outhouses and a large garden overlooking flat but lovely countryside.

The local residents were none too pleased by this intrusion, and matters might have gone awry for the family had it not been for Mr O'Rourke's almost uncanny abilities as a handyman. He could, it seemed, mend literally everything, and he was soon the most popular man in the village. He fixed cars, washing-machines, videos and vacuum cleaners with equal panache, and he would as cheerfully programme a word-processor as mow a lawn. Where this skill came from, he himself does not know; perhaps his keen eye for detail and wide reading were the reason, or perhaps he had the mechanical equivalent of green fingers. Whatever the reason, he became an invaluable part of the community. People wondered quite seriously how they had managed to get along without this astonishing family. Mrs O'Rourke, not to be outdone, was so experienced in cooking and taking care of children that she was soon the boon companion of every woman in the village. With permission, Mr O'Rourke converted an outhouse into an unobtrusive repair shop that sold all those things that other shops seem to have forgotten about. Tap washers, batteries, spare parts for cars, anything that you might need in an emergency, you could find at Paddy's Place, as his home came to be affectionately known. He was soon able to install a telephone, buy a secondhand van and start to put a little money aside.

It was almost exactly six months after they moved in

that Mrs O'Rourke's third youngest, a boy called Declan, told his mother of the strange man he had seen in his room. A devout Catholic, she explained that it was his Guardian Angel, who made himself visible from time to time just to show that he was still at his post. The boy was perfectly satisfied, but she was slightly perturbed to hear the same story from the eldest boy only an hour after he had returned from a fortnight at a summer camp, before he had a chance to speak to his brother. A week later she saw the apparition herself, walking slowly along the front hall; when it smiled at her, she crossed herself, but she says that the action was purely reflex, as she felt no fear whatsoever. Quite the contrary, as the spirit seemed to exude an aura of safety and wholesomeness. Mr O'Rourke saw him a little later the same day on the upstairs landing and mistook him for a customer sent up by his wife, only to be astounded by the figure's disappearing before his eyes. He too, however, reports that there was none of the terror one has been taught to associate with seeing a ghost, and its later appearances in various parts of the house occasioned no comment.

Half way through September Geraldine, the eldest of the girls, complained of feeling unwell and was put to bed. She fell into a fitful sleep during the humid afternoon and seemed little better when she awoke. The weather had been excessively warm for a long time, and during the evening it broke. The resulting storm was one of the worst ever experienced in that part of the country, with torrential rain, vivid lightning and tremendous thunder. It was one of those storms that circled a particular region, at one time seeming to go away, only to return later with what appeared to be renewed vigour. Suddenly Geraldine became rapidly worse, and Mr O'Rourke decided to telephone for a doctor from the nearby town. To his horror, the phone was out of order, as were all the phones in the village. He tried to drive the van, but the rain was coming down so hard that the wipers could not clear the screen, and it would have been lethal to go out onto the roads. Then there was a power-cut, and the family had to struggle to find two old paraffin lamps for temporary lighting.

There was no nurse or retired doctor in the village, and the O'Rourkes were thrown entirely on their own resources. The child's temperature was 101° and rising, and they struggled to keep it from going higher with cold bandages wrapped around her head. For all their efforts, Geraldine was obviously getting worse, and the couple knelt by the sickbed in silent prayer. Mrs O'Rourke remembers hearing a slight rustling sound and, looking up, she saw the figure of the phantom looking down at the tossing figure on the bed. Using a sign-language of gestures, he indicated that Mr O'Rourke should follow him, which he did without hesitation. (The couple both report that they no longer regarded him as anything other than someone sent by God in answer to their prayers.) The spirit leading, they reached the second reception room, which was kept in the traditional way as the room in which honoured guests were entertained, and never used by the family. The figure turned and pointed to an ornamental panel set in the wall, indicating that one of the decorative buttons was to be pressed to the left. As Mr O'Rourke did so, the panel swung open to reveal a small but amply filled medicine cabinet. The finger then pointed out a hypodermic syringe and a vial of some medicine.

Mr O'Rourke's encyclopaedic knowledge had never stood him in better stead: following the advice of the spirit, he filled the syringe to the mark indicated and followed him back to the bedroom. He was then instructed to up-end the syringe and squirt off a small amount to expel any air; then the pointing finger told him where to make the injection, and the operation was over. All three stood there until the restless figure on the bed became still and peaceful.

The O'Rourkes cannot remember how long they stood, but they were brought to themselves by the light of dawn shining through the curtains. Their mysterious friend had vanished, and Geraldine's temperature had gone down.

For some months after that the ghost, or whatever he was, was still visible but gradually declining in clarity, although they would often catch glimpses of him in the wintry garden and on the stairs. To them he was a respected member of the family, and they saluted him with every courtesy. Woe betide the child who failed to speak respectfully or didn't acknowledge him as he passed. Finally he was gone for good, and a blankness fell over the family as it would if one of its living members were to go away. He is constantly in their prayers, and a candle burns continually in their local church, the only reminder there still is of the ghost who came back to save a child's life.

Later it was discovered that a doctor had formerly lived in the house. He had had a fear of burglars stealing drugs and had had the compartment constructed for the safe-keeping of all pharmaceuticals and instruments. He had died too suddenly to leave instructions for their disposal.

The secret compartment is now a grotto or, some may say, a shrine. In it, a photo of the doctor discovered in the attic shares pride of place with a statue of the Blessed Virgin Mary, both testifying in their own way to our lack of knowledge of the nature of the universe.

The O'Rourkes are one of the nicest families one could hope to meet, and they have not squandered the opportunities given them. For those who would like to know more of this delightful family, I have permission to give the following information.

Geraldine is studying to be a doctor, and the three younger girls are either trainee nurses or planning to be when they finish their education.

Mr O'Rourke has been a great success and now has two other shops in outlying areas, managed by his eldest sons. He still works tirelessly for village people but also finds time to run a mail-order spares business and to contribute a weekly DIY article to the local newspaper.

Mrs O'Rourke, now relieved of many of the pressing duties of looking after a young family, teaches cookery and child care at the local nightschool and is highly regarded for her poetry, a talent which has had a chance to blossom only in recent years.

The O'Rourkes have bought their wonderful house from the council on a mortgage, and it is now their turn to be benefactors of those who are less fortunate than themselves. They take a number of underprivileged children every year and give them a holiday in their home.

An Odd Miscellany I

Many readers may have been gracious enough to notice that the reports in this book have not been filled with extraneous detail. To use the crude vernacular of my own profession, they haven't been 'padded'. The incidents I shall relate in this and the other 'miscellany' sections all raise profound questions, but much extra material would have to be used to make them individual stories worthy of separate titles. Nevertheless, it is only in length that they differ – the 'inexplicable' content is as great, if not greater, than in the titled narratives.

'The Dripping Man of the Fens' is a well-known figure from Lincolnshire down to Suffolk. He's been seen by couples, groups, parties of schoolchildren etc, and there can be no doubt that he exists. What he is is a different matter. Whether it is day or night, hot or cold, wet or dry, this strange man always appears along the coast dressed in a sort of oilcloth jacket, dark trousers and sou'wester. He is always reported in the same way: a man, clearly upset, who has recently been immersed in water, because his clothes are still dripping profusely. He hurries up to people and always asks the same question, 'Have you seen my boy?' People respond compassionately and ask for more details, or volunteer to help him look, and his response is always the same: a weary shake of the head, then he is off again. Sometimes he has been reported over an entire hot afternoon at different times, but always dripping wet, and still without his boy.

He would not seem to be a mirage of any sort, or a straightforward ghost, because he leaves behind pools of water wherever he stands, and is in all respects just like a normal person. That he is not just an eccentric is vouched for by the fact that he has been seen (to my knowledge) for over a century. There is a small piece about him in a now defunct paper that served parts of the Fens in 1878, and even then the reporter talks of him as though he were already well known.

I should be grateful if any reader who knows of any press reports prior to that date would get in touch with me via the publisher.

The curious experience of the Lange family when they were driving through Wales in 1961 raises not just one problem and, like so many of these weird things, is not without parallels in many countries and many times.

The family had decided to go on a tour of Wales, using a caravan. The party consisted of Alistair and Mary Lange, and two of their children, Sandra and Selina. The eldest, Samantha (aged seventeen), who had a frightful cold, was staying at home to continue her A-level studies and to look after the youngest, Sheila.

They had spent a week of the holiday most enjoyably and were planning a further two days in North Wales before returning home to Shropshire. The weather had worsened during the afternoon, and the night was an unpleasant one for driving. As they passed a small village, they came to a long stretch of road that led to a large town in which they could camp with some amenities. Halfway down this dismal thoroughfare there was a policeman standing in the middle of the road with a lamp, clearly there to stop them. Alistair pulled over to the side of the road and wound the window down. The policeman, a constable with a peaked cap, came up and asked if he was called Lange. Alarmed, Alistair replied in the affirmative, and the policeman told him that they had had a report of an accident at his home. He assured the frightened parents that no injuries were known to have been sustained, but advised them to return at once.

The parents' first thought was to get to a phone, then back home as soon as possible. In all they found five phones, but not one was usable for one reason or the other. Two were kiosks out of order, one was at a garage that said its line was down due to the winds, another was at a cottage whose owner declined to open the door, and the last was at a pub where they were rudely told they could use the telephone only if they bought a meal. Alistair offered to pay for four meals and not have them in return for one phone call, but the publican wouldn't hear of it. Mary was by now frantic, and as it would take less than an hour to drive direct, they decided not to waste any more time but to get home immediately.

Upon arriving they found the house lights still on, and no trouble of any sort. Samantha was hard at work and was mystified. She had made no calls of any kind, let alone an emergency one, and the whole house was in perfect order. The parents were irate by this time and decided to call the police in that part of Wales to demand an explanation.

As Alistair went into the hall to call the station, he detected the smell of gas at the foot of the stairs. It was definitely coming from above, and he rushed to the youngest girl's bedroom to bring her to safety, first alerting the rest of the family to evacuate the house and to call the fire brigade from a neighbour's house. Sheila was perfectly all right, and the authorities soon traced and repaired the leak from a water-heater. The British Gas repairman congratulated Alistair on discovering it so early, as an upstairs leak is the most dangerous, the gas accumulating in large quantities before anyone notices. Samantha had a bad cold and might not have noticed the gas, which would quite quickly have killed Sheila, then ignited – probably to kill Samantha and the people living on both sides. *Had the parents been able to get through on the phone, they would have been told there was no danger and would not have returned to prevent it.*

Alistair did phone the Welsh police the next day and was told that they had sent out no officer to stop anyone. He also made a complaint to the brewery about the landlord of the pub (which seems a bit ungrateful, given the result), having taken the man's name from over the pub door. The brewery had a pub of the name he mentioned, but its landlord was a lady.

There seems no logical explanation for this sort of thing. If the spirit – the 'policeman' – knew about the gas and was capable of waving lamps about, why didn't it phone British Gas? It is possible that Alistair was confused about the names on the pub door or had gone to a different pub. It is also possible to strike a long line of non-working phones (don't we all know it). But the overall atmosphere of the story suggests something so mysterious that we cannot even begin to grapple with it.

There were many witnesses to the last story, and with this one we have three. Indeed, if one is not prepared to take somebody's word somewhere along the line, all investigation, whether it be into routine crime or psychic happenings, becomes a nonsense.

Animals often feature in stories of the occult, it being an article of faith that they are better at detecting ghosts than human beings. If this is true, and some evidence seems to support it, why are they frightened so terribly even of ghosts who are benign? Animals probably do not have the concept of death in the abstract, merely responses to danger. Many animal-loving readers will disagree with this, and I am not sure I wholly believe it, being a great devotee of cats. Nevertheless, I think it is only conditioning that makes us scared of ghosts, much the same as a modern child is scared of the dentist, through a sort of folklore.

Animals meet all sorts of inexplicable phenomena in their lives. Their master – or, in the case of a cat, their slave – raises his hand to a wall, and the world is flooded with light. He points a stick at a box, and flashing colours and loud noises fill the room. My own cat has walked along my word-processor's keyboard and heard strange bleeps and seen lights flash, yet she bats not an eyelid.

Good and evil barely exist, even to human beings; our world is based largely on a pain-pleasure, threat-gift principle, so how much more does this apply to animals?

We hear that Lord Caernarvon's dogs barked the night he died in Cairo after pillaging the grave of King Tut, but perhaps they growled quite often – dogs will. Nevertheless, animals sometimes act in a way that makes us think that they are in touch with a deeper reality than we are.

This was the case with Arthur Walker's collie. They worked a small farm almost as a human duo, Davy the dog showing extraordinary flair in helping with many more tasks than one would associate even with the best-trained sheepdog. He would, for instance, sort the mail out into envelopes with panels, the type that contains bills, and letters with stamps. Normally he would bring both sets to Arthur, but if his master was in a bad mood, Davy would keep the bills back until good humour had returned.

I have said some things that might seem disparaging about animals, but their faults are minor compared to the follies of man. For no apparent reason, Davy took it into his head to prevent Arthur from going into a small paddock by the side of the house. He would bark and jump up, doing everything but bite in his desperate efforts to keep Arthur out. Arthur talked to his friends about it at the local pub, and one idiot suggested that he should teach the dog a lesson by doping its food and going into the paddock and staying there until the dog awoke both literally and metaphorically to the superiority of the human species. Arthur was unkind enough and foolish enough to take the advice, and some of his nastier neighbours came with him to see the 'fun'. The dog was given something with his evening meal and was soon fast asleep.

The man who did not deserve a dog, let alone Davy, walked into the field and was struck dead by lightning from a cloudless sky; an unusual but not unknown phenomenon.

George Meddowes had inherited a small business from his father and turned it into a great one. He was surrounded by all the trappings of wealth, and all the responsibilities. One of these was that he had to fly all over the world on business trips. He hated the major airlines and used his own private plane for shorter journeys.

On one occasion he was flying to France with his best friend at the controls. They had been to school together and served in the same regiment, and now Jack Davies was senior pilot and minor shareholder in his friend's company. There was one other person aboard, a junior secretary who doubled as a sort of air hostess. The plane took off towards France, with an estimated flying-time of just over two hours. That would give George ample time for a decent dinner and an early night before the meeting in the morning. He was dictating some rough notes to the secretary, Pauline Barnes, when there was a crash from the pilot's cabin. Pauline hurried to investigate and returned to report. 'He's very ill,' she said.

George rushed into the small compartment. His friend was obviously close to death, and George cradled him in his arms. Jack's eyes opened momentarily and he smiled. He whispered, 'I haven't forgotten the big Chink,' and then he died. George half dragged, half carried his friend back into the office, laying him gently on the camp bed. He felt a deep sense of desolation at the loss of a man who had been at his side for as long as he could remember. The cryptic final words added a poignancy to his sorrow. When they were young officers in Korea, George had saved Jack's life by wrestling to the ground, and strangling, a Chinese soldier who was about to bayonet his friend to death. He got up from the bed and placed his jacket over his friend's face.

It was only then that their situation really came home to him. The pilot was dead and he knew nothing whatsoever about aircraft. Unless Miss Barnes had been taking secret lessons, they were goners. 'Can you ...?' she asked, and he shook his head, her question answering his. They looked out of the window; tiny twinkling lights far below testified to the distance they had to fall.

As they watched, the lights went out, as cloud built up below them, and lightning replaced the man-made illumination. The plane began to buck and twist in the force of the storm. George couldn't use the plane's radio, but they tried the radio-phone – only static came from it. He had had a fanciful idea of getting in contact with a pilot and receiving instructions on how to land the plane but, in his heart, he knew that such things belonged only in the field of romantic fiction. He assumed that the plane was on automatic pilot, but how long it could stay stable in the storm was anybody's guess. However long, the inevitable running-out of fuel would mark the end.

Miss Barnes got them both some whisky, and they slipped into their private reveries. It seemed so strange – the plane was well lit and warm, a whole range of food and drink was at their disposal, yet they were as surely dead as if they were trapped in a black cave under a mountain. Inevitably George's thoughts went back to the war in Korea, and the time when he had grappled with the Chinese soldier in order to save his friend.

It took him a few seconds to become aware of it, but the plane had steadied, although the storm still flashed outside. A fluke, he thought, but it persisted, and the plane was going down – not headlong, as he expected, but in the gentle slope he had so often experienced. Pauline was standing now, as familiar with the difference between landing and diving as he was. They looked into the cabin and saw the controls moving surely and steadily as if under the control of a guiding intelligence. The light came on to tell them to fasten their belts, and the plane made an unscheduled but perfect landing.

MALEVOLENT GHOSTS

A Well-meaning Spirit!

This haunting, if that is the right word, is one of the most peculiar on record. It is, however, not unique. The prankster ghost turns up occasionally, and I know of two other cases in relatively recent times, but this one is a much more advanced example of the type, and the spirit shows a remarkable facility in using the equipment in our world (a telephone and alarm clock, for instance). The final conversation it has with Janet Burnett is quite sad in its way, and we have to wonder if we do not have some sort of occult 'crying clown'. I should like to make a few points when the story is over as, like so many of this kind of visitation, the spirit does not seem to have a full grip on the situation, and there is a childlike, rather than childish, aspect to many of its actions, but with adult behaviour breaking in from time to time. Whether the phantom could actually see the future or made educated guesses must be decided by the reader.

The Burnetts are a prosperous youngish couple, John an executive with a multinational oil company, Janet a freelance photographer. At the time of these events they lived in a flat on the borders of St John's Wood. Neither had any interest in psychic matters or that group of phenomena we call 'the Unexplained', for want of a better word. They were Anglicans more by habit and a hazy belief than by strong conviction, and neither of them had had any unusual experiences of the paranormal in any shape or form.

On the Friday on which these weird happenings were to begin, Janet was at home preparing for a dinner party that evening. John's immediate superior and his wife were coming round for a meal and to look the flat over, an identical one having become available elsewhere in the block. Janet had a woman from a catering agency to help with the food and to assist generally in making it a splendid turn-out, although it wasn't intended to be a very formal party, and Janet had not taken advantage of the waiting service offered. The firm would simply call the next morning to clear up.

Janet had explained in detail what she wanted, then left on an assignment. She came back two hours later to find a note from the woman saying that she had gone back to base for some of the special items Janet required, which she couldn't find in the house. Janet went to inspect the layout in the dining-room and was annoyed to find that the table had been set for five, not four. The woman arrived back a few minutes later and expressed equal surprise. She was, she said, a professional of some ten years experience, and if she was told a party was for four, four settings she prepared. However, since no one else could have laid it, she apologized and the extra place was removed.

About three John rang to say that there had been an unexpected change of plans. Their guest's wife's mother had arrived unexpectedly from America, and it seemed impolite to let the lady fend for herself. Would it be OK if they made dinner for five? It wasn't a problem and struck Janet as no more than a mild coincidence that five places had been set by mistake.

The mother turned out to be a positive adornment to the party, being a born raconteuse, with many amusing stories from her transatlantic wanderings. They were having coffee when John commented on how hot the weather had become. It was early April, but very warm for the season.

'What we need is a good shower of rain,' commented the lady from America, and almost instantly water began to pour from the ceiling, drenching everybody.

Janet leapt up, thinking a pipe had burst. She ran to the door and was astonished to see the 'rain' starting about a foot below the ceiling, and falling only on the guests, the remainder of the room remaining perfectly dry. The others left the table hurriedly and grouped themselves by Janet, watching the uncanny event from safety. Then it stopped, leaving the table and food drenched. It was quite late and the party broke up, everyone puzzled and a little frightened. As people do when faced with the inexplicable, John offered a rational explanation: he suggested that the steam from the kettle used for the coffee, and the excessive humidity of the room, had caused a minor precipitation of excess moisture. This was a very thin explanation, as all the coffee cups had been filled to overflowing during the minute or so it had 'rained', but at least it was something to hang on to.

The next day Janet had two early appointments, and John was booked for some golf. They had tea and sandwiches at about five and decided to go to the pictures, a fairly common relaxation for both of them. The cinema was packed, as the film had been widely acclaimed. Half way through there appeared on the screen one of those messages sent by putting a small dark piece of film with the words scratched on it over the projector. It said, 'WILL MR & MRS BURNETT PLEASE GO TO THE MANAGER'S OFFICE.' Janet's mother was unwell at the time, and they were both concerned that she might have taken a turn for the worse. The manager was most courteous and told them that one of his staff had received a message, somewhat garbled, concerning their home and a fire. They hurried back but found everything normal. Their neighbours knew nothing of it, and the fire brigade were equally in the dark about any alarm being raised. Cursing the stupidity of the hoaxer, they watched some TV and went to bed early. When they went out to their local pub at midday on Sunday for their usual drinks and lunch, they passed the cinema, only to find it boarded up and smoke-blackened. At the pub it was common knowledge that the place had caught fire during the evening performance, and more than thirty people had been taken to hospital suffering from smoke inhalation or injuries received in the panic rush to escape.

John recalls thanking their lucky stars that some fool had dragged them away on a wild goose chase before the accident; Janet, however, says she had a curious feeling about the incident, coming, as it did, so close after the funny events at the dinner party, and she remembers John commenting on her subdued manner.

The next afternoon John's secretary phoned, full of apologies. He had asked her to buy some of Janet's favourite chocolates, and she admitted that she had forgotten what they were, even though it was an errand she had done a couple of times before. 'Oh, get me some "Roses", please,' Janet replied, hoping that her mood of the previous day had not made him think he had upset her in any way. She went down to the shops to stock up after the dinner party, had a coffee with some friends and got back just after three. On the mat was a gorgeous bunch of red roses with her name but no message. John was determined to spoil her, she thought, and she went into the kitchen to return the compliment by cooking him his favourite meal. He arrived home about seven, carrying the tin of chocolates. He looked at the flowers. 'Got a secret admirer?' he joked, only to frown when she explained that she thought he had sent them.

Over dinner they decided that their guests of Friday must be the mysterious donors, and Janet phoned to thank them, but they hadn't sent them. Then the memory of her conversation with the secretary came back to her. She had said, 'Get me some roses, please,' and roses had appeared, just as the rain had fallen when it was asked for. She suddenly felt quite afraid, and voiced her fears to her husband. Wasn't it odd, she queried, that two wishes should be granted and that they should be lured away from the cinema just before a fire broke out? It seemed as if their conversations were being overheard, which would explain roses (the flowers) for 'Roses' (the chocolates). John pooh-poohed the idea as nothing more than a coincidence, but she had the bit between her teeth.

'Let's ask Jim and Samantha about it. It can't do any harm, can it?'

He nodded reluctantly. 'If it'll make you feel better, I'll ring them now.'

Jim and Samantha were two old friends, much into Spiritualism, alternative medicine and similar things. It was John's belief that they were cranks, fun in small doses but a bit outside the sort of people he liked to associate with on a regular basis.

Scenting something unusual, the couple were round

like a shot. They both nodded excitedly as the tale unfolded, and enthusiastically suggested a seance with a ouija board. In for a penny, in for a pound, John helped cut up the pieces of paper and write the letters of the alphabet on them – there were also two pieces for YES and NO, and a wine-glass completed the ensemble.

Janet and John sat with their friends, feeling rather self-conscious as the ritual question 'Is there anybody there?' was intoned by Samantha. The glass moved suddenly towards 'YES. Jim asked for the spirit's name, but it stayed where it was. Then Janet overcame her reserve and asked why it was there. Very quickly the glass spelt out 'TO HELP YOU'.

Like many sceptics in the face of even a minimum of evidence, John became a believer instantly. 'Did you send the flowers and the rain?' he almost shouted. The glass went to 'YES', and the atmosphere became electric.

Jim asked the spirit when it had died, getting the reply 'I'M NOT DEAD.' He tried a different tack. 'Who were you before you became what you are now?' The glass remained stock still.

Samantha waded in with, 'Did you have a body like ours once?' It shot around the table spelling out 'NOT LIKE YOURS', then it tipped on one side, then righted itself with a loud tap, almost as if it were an exclamation mark. As Samantha was a most beautiful woman, this might be considered an occult equivalent of a wolf-whistle.

'Have you anything to tell us?' asked John, now fully in the spirit of the seance. 'SORRY ABOUT THE RAIN,' was spelt out.

Nobody at the table doubted that some sort of external intelligence was moving the glass; it went almost too fast for them to read the letters, and yet no pressure was felt by anyone and, anyway, even two people acting in concert cannot make a glass move convincingly.

A lot of inconsequential questions were asked, and some quite pertinent ones. Generally the glass refused to move when a serious query was put. The spirit admitted sending the message to the cinema, adding its name for good measure, but refused to be drawn on how it knew what was to come. Janet asked who was going to win the coming election and got the seemingly inane reply, 'RUSHES UP TO THE ROOF', only later realizing that it could be seen as a pun on the name (or rather the job of a) Thatcher. In response to a lack of questions, the glass rapidly spelt out 'HE'S NOT TIRED BUT I AM' and rushed across the table with such force that it landed in Jim's lap. No further movement could be got from the glass when it was replaced, and they had coffee and discussed the puzzling business until quite late.

Only when Jim and Samantha went out to drive home did the last part of the message take on a relevance. Their car was standing on bricks, all the wheels having been removed, not an uncommon experience in that neighbourhood, which adjoined some of the roughest areas of North London. Once again it could have been a coincidence, but 'HE'S NOT TIRED' said to a man whose wheels – tyres – have been stolen from his car is quite something to explain away. Instead of being angry, the two Spiritualists seemed to consider it the end of a perfect day, going home by minicab only after extracting a promise that they would be kept abreast of all events.

When they were in bed, John suddenly remembered an important telephone call he had to make the next afternoon. He had left his diary in the car, so he said to Janet, whose memory was a byword, 'Give me a ring about four. I've got to call Simmonds rather urgently.' Rather drowsily she answered, 'OK.' The next thing they remember is being awakened at four in the morning by the alarm clock. John struggled up cursing but had no sooner silenced the thing and got back into bed when the telephone rang. Janet's mother was still very poorly, so it brought them both to full consciousness. It turned out to be an alarm-call operator, well used to irascible people, who could give no information on who had booked the early call.

John was apologetic, conceding that Janet had been right from the start: something well-meaning *was* listening in and trying to do the right thing, but generally getting it wrong. Although they felt in no danger from the presence life rapidly became impossible. Using the bathroom was an embarrassment, Janet flatly refused to undress with the light on, and neither had any inclination towards lovemaking.

Reluctantly they decided to call in the minister from their local church to conduct a service of exorcism, and Janet called at the vicarage to arrange it. He was a young priest, and it was his first such request. To Janet, he seemed very lukewarm, but he promised to call later that evening. He arrived just after eight. The party included Jim and Samantha, as had been promised, although they were against the exorcism. There were, they protested, too few examples of genuine spirit manifestations, and when they did occur, they should be investigated thoroughly. Janet, however, was quite adamant, and the service began.

The minister had barely uttered the first few words when an unseen hand opened the Bible he had placed on a table, and began tearing out the pages. These were flung and began to form a slowly circling nimbus around the cowering clergyman's head. From there they gravitated towards the table, coming to rest spelling out 'GO AWAY.' Jim and Samantha were hugging themselves with glee, and John and Janet could hardly repress a smile at the incongruous scene. Only the minister, ashen-faced and panting, seemed out of place. As soon as the halo had disappeared, he made a bolt for the door, leaving the rest of them in various states of amusement or delight.

When John had left for work, Janet decided she had to do something or have their lives ruined by this uninvited guest. She went into the living-room and said very loudly, 'I wish you were here to be spoken to.' It may have been imagination, she said later, but she did seem to sense someone else in the room. 'I'm sorry to have to speak to you like this,' she went on, 'but although I know you mean to help us, and be kind, that isn't the effect you're having.' She paused, unsure of herself. 'What I mean is, you are wrecking our marriage and taking away our peace of mind. We can look after ourselves, you know – we always have before, and knowing that you're about, watching and listening, is making us very miserable. If it goes on, we shan't be able to sleep or work, and everything we've worked for will be ruined.'

In the corner of the room there began to appear what

looked like a wisp of cigar smoke; it grew more dense, until the outline of a person was just detectable, but whether it was male or female was impossible to tell. Janet says she experienced a momentary pang of fear, but the vibrations from whatever it was were so gentle and benign that it faded almost as soon as it started, and she continued with more confidence now that there was something to talk to.

'We don't know how things work in your world, and whether you're unhappy. Our friends say that you may be an earthbound soul, unable to get away – if we can help, we will. There are things called rescue circles we can join to give you the strength you need, and we will pray for you – all the time – every day, because we know you're kind.'

The smoke seemed to be dissolving but, before it went for good, she heard a voice – a soft, sighing voice – that she is not sure whether she heard with her ears or her mind: 'Thank you. It would be nice if you said prayers. I think they would help.' The corner was empty then, and she remembers that a feeling of total exhaustion came over her, as well as a sense of loss.

Until this day Janet is still in doubt about whether she did the right thing. Was there a different approach she could have used that would have been more help? They still pray, on their knees, once a day for that spirit, and they are long-term members of the local Spiritualist church, taking an especial interest in rescue circles. The spirit has never come to one of their meetings, and Janet hopes that, whatever it was, it is now at peace.

That this actually occurred as reported, there can be no doubt. Unbeknown to Janet and John, I checked with the florist, and a bunch of roses with no message was delivered to that address on the day stipulated.

Although the spirit saved them from injury and possible death in the cinema, what is curious is that it did not make any effort to warn all those other people who were injured.

A report on the fire stated that it had been smouldering for a long time, perhaps even from the night before, so by stretching the imagination we can visualize a disembodied spirit finding out about it. Likewise, it could have found out by normal means that the lady was coming back from America. (These suppositions require a lot of 'ifs', but there isn't an example of the spirit's actually knowing something in advance that could not have been researched, like being struck by lightning, for example.

Mrs Thatcher's victory was highly probable, if in fact that is what was meant by the reply. I was at a seance once when a spirit was questioned about the future; it replied, very sensibly, I thought, 'WHY SHOULD I KNOW JUST BECAUSE I'VE LEFT MY BODY BEHIND?')

A normal person would know that John didn't want to phone someone up at four in the morning. Even if he had, he would not ask a person just going to sleep to remind him.

How did it manage to cause water to materialize from nowhere at will? This sort of thing has happened before, but that only adds to the mystery; it doesn't explain it.

Why did it want to help *them* in particular, and why didn't it warn of the robbery of the wheels, rather than simply make a bad pun?

Was it pleased to have prayers said, or was it simply being polite? Certainly, its motives seem to have been pure, because it went when it realized that it could help more by going than by staying.

A Terrifying Phantom

Alec Porter was a professional restorer of old houses. This had been his business since he was in his early twenties, and served as both a source of income and a hobby.

The process is now known as 'gentrification' and has received a bad press of recent years because it has involved buying up property in poor areas, making it look beautiful, then selling it for an astronomical sum to the new rich of Mrs Thatcher's Britain. This causes a lot of resentment as the houses are totally outside the range of those who have lived in the area all their lives, and whose children have to move far afield to find cheaper accommodation. Whatever the rights and wrongs of the system, Alec operated in less uneasy times and rarely encountered hostility.

Having received a small inheritance before the war, he concentrated on cottages in pretty villages not far from main roads or railway stations, and sold them to what were then called the 'idle rich', 'bright young things' and 'flappers'. After the war there was a great deal of property going cheap, but with the twin impediments of government restrictions and a noticeable absence of the free-spending youngsters who had largely provided Alec's living, things were not as easy as they had been before. Nevertheless, he found enough buyers to make a good income. All people who buy things for a living have a secret dream – the Chippendale being used as a tool chest, the Turner blocking a draught from window: each profession has its secret hope of Eldorado. With Alec it was less well defined, but he knew he would know it when he saw it.

In 1969, a year before he had decided to retire, he found it. A run-down farmhouse of considerable size, standing in an astonishing twenty-six acres of good land, with woods and a lake. The price being asked was quite remarkably low, and he looked around for the snag. It did not take long to discover it was the commonest of all: the house was reputedly haunted. He would have liked a shilling for every place he had heard that about, and he did not see it as a drawback to his plans. With exterior lights, a landscaped garden and new windows in a refurbished wall, the place would quickly lose any aura of mystery with the villagers, and no outside buyer would think twice about snapping it up.

The ghost, or ghosts, were said to consist of strange lights seen at windows during the night, and a black figure of immense size who sometimes stalked the surrounding lanes. There were also reports of loud and inexplicable noises being heard at all hours of the day. To Alec, it was a textbook case, but it had sufficiently scared off any tenants for more than thirty years. Nevertheless, he felt sure that he could make an excellent profit, enough to enable him to retire in comfort.

He hired as much labour locally as he could, and found that with work in short supply there was not too much reluctance to come in, although the men preferred an early start and an early finish to running the risk of being still around the place when darkness fell. Slowly, however, close contact with the place was having an effect in dispelling the miasma of fear that surrounded the decaying house.

After a couple of weeks, when Alec moved from clearing the wildly overgrown gardens to the house itself, some strange things did start to happen, all the more frightening because they seemed to have him as the target. On one occasion, a heavy concrete flower bowl, which he had checked for safety the day before, crashed down, missing his head by inches and cracking two of his toes. He was at pains to minimize the significance of this, announcing that nobody was to approach the house until other loose fixtures had been either removed or made secure. Later on, he took a look at the pedestal on which the bowl had stood. Its base was over a foot square, and the bowl's height a mere thirty inches, making the centre of gravity very low. It was certain, therefore, that a great deal of force must have been exercised to make it topple from such a secure foundation. Not being a great believer in the supernatural, although not an out-and-out sceptic, he wondered whether someone wasn't out to scupper the whole enterprise. This seemed very fanciful, and murder was still a crime for which one could be hanged. Perhaps he hadn't been as scrupulous in checking the bowl as he thought. On another occasion, he nearly had a serious accident when he stepped on some newspaper, only to find that one of the floorboards had been removed. Generally, however, things went along normally enough.

It was clear that the shell of the building and the foundations were very sound; what was needed was for most of the interior walls to be removed and replaced by designs that were more in keeping with the modern style. Alec measured all the rooms on each of the three floors and, leaving instructions with the foreman for further clearance of the grounds, went back to London to study the complex plans and to have the new interior drafted by a firm of architects he had used for years.

Two days later, there was a call from the foreman (an old employee of Alec's, and not from the village) to say that there was a lot of crashing and banging coming from inside the house and that the men had downed tools. Could he have the keys to go in and examine the place? Alec pointed out that it wasn't locked, as there was nothing worth stealing; if there *was* anything valuable about the place, it was the tarpaulins, bricks and sundries now stored outside the house. The foreman was back on the phone a few minutes later – not a door would open, even when encouraged to by a good hard kick. As it had rained the night before, Alec suggested that perhaps the old wood had swollen and needed to be prised away from the jambs. The foreman sounded less than convinced by this idea but said he would have a go. He telephoned back a half-hour later to report that the noise had stopped and that all the doors were now working. That left the problem of an absent workforce, and Alec promised to be up the next day to see what could be done. If the worst came to the worst, he could hire coaches in the nearby town and bus men into work, but this would only reinforce the sinister reputation the house had already acquired.

The architects telephoned to tell him that the measurement of the rooms were all wrong, and could they call round. The discrepancy lay on the first floor, where the sizes of the rooms added together were considerably less than either the width or length of the property. A space was left in the centre, about twenty-five feet square, which seemed unlikely as there were no points of entry or exit in any of the surrounding rooms. As Alec had himself taken all the measurements, he rather inclined to the idea that there was a hidden room. If the room did exist, perhaps it contained empty wine casks or other easily moved objects which rolled about from time to time, causing the noise. Why they should do so in a closed environment, he had no idea, but the whole thing was getting on his nerves. Perhaps, he now remembers, the memory of the cement flower bowl nearly smashing him to a pulp was preying on his mind.

He arrived on the site early, to be met by the foreman, an old soldier whose nerves seemed to be non-existent.

Telling him to bring a pickaxe with him, Alec led the way to one of the rooms on the first floor and asked him to knock a hole in the wall. A few strong blows soon knocked a small aperture in the ancient stonework, enough to shine a torch through. The beam picked the bare laths on the far wall, and he gradually moved it around the room. On the right-hand side it encountered a tall black object that reflected no light. As soon as the beam touched it, a shrill chattering noise began, like that of a monkeyhouse, only much louder. He withdrew the light with a start and retreated instinctively.

The noise seemed to intensify, and from the hole a black vapour began to emerge, bringing with it a stink of such awfulness that they recoiled nearly vomiting. Although there were cracked windows and an open door with a fresh breeze blowing through it, the smoke did not dissipate but began to curl upwards, growing denser as it did so. As they watched, it seemed to form a grotesquely misshapen head, and what seemed to be two arms began to develop at its shoulders. They both felt an overpowering sense of evil from the thing and, almost in panic, rushed for the stairs, the foreman losing his balance in his frantic rush and breaking his arm in the resulting fall. Undeterred, or not feeling the excruciating pain, he was on his feet in an instant and bounding for the door, his employer close at his heels. Once in the open air they felt better and turned to look again at the place they had so recently vacated, only to see it standing there as innocuously as a vicarage. Alec took the foreman to a hospital, then drove back to London, still badly shaken by the frightening experience.

It is a curious fact of human nature, well chronicled over the ages, that money will overcome most things, and it was no less true for Alec than for anyone else. Putting the story to a scientific friend, he found himself heartily chastised for his cowardice and credulity. The room, he was told, was probably a modification of the old Roman idea of a *vomitarium*, a place for the escape of smoke and kitchen vapours. The final storey was added later, and chimneys were built all around the 'secret' room. Over the years, soot had built up in very large quantities, perhaps gathering around some pillar put in to shore up the second floor. Although there were no chinks of light, birds

had undoubtedly found their way into such a safe refuge
and were the cause of the noise when the light was shone
around the room. Breezes blowing in from both window
and door had caused a small vortex or whirlwind to
develop which had sucked out the soot and made it whirl
upwards into the shape they had imagined to be an evil
spirit. The awful smell was a compound of all kinds of rot,
and perhaps centuries of bird-droppings. Quite likely,
Alec's friend added, the flapping of birds disturbed by the
workmen in the confined space had caused the resonating
sound the foreman had reported.

Because there was so much money involved and partly
because he was ashamed of his behaviour, Alec decided to
have one last try. Curiously, he admits now, he tried to
hedge his bets, taking with him a crucifix that had belonged
to his grandmother, a devout Catholic. He made a point of
getting there at noon, and gingerly went up to the room. All
was quiet, and he began to find his courage seeping back.
Holding the crucifix in front of his face, he approached the
hole in the wall, whispering some words he had heard from
a horror film when a man was in a similar situation: 'If you
be Devil, I command you to go, in the name of Our Lord
Jesus Christ.' What had been total silence was suddenly
blasted by the most incredible noises – the tolling of a great
bell, and what sounded like the tramp of huge feet. Then
something pushed him over onto the floor, and a great
bellowing voice roared out a torrent of blasphemous obsce-
nities. Terrified, he tried to struggle up, only to see his
crucifix hanging suspended in mid-air. As he watched, the
image of Christ was ripped from the wood and, in an
unmistakable gesture, the little brass figure was pulled
back like a dart about to be thrown. He threw himself to one
side, but the hurtling missile struck his arm, burying itself
deep in the flesh. Gibbering with terror, he half crawled,
half stumbled towards the door, while the tolling of the bell
seemed to grow louder.

He cannot remember getting to his car and driving
away, but he managed to get help for his injured arm
some hours later, about four o'clock, a hundred miles from
the scene. When he was feeling calmer, he gave orders
that the property was to be sold. He never wished to set

eyes on it again.

Alec *has* a prominent scar where he said the figure of Christ struck him. However, I was a little sceptical because, by chance, I knew that area slightly, having known a girl from there, whom I used to meet at a pub in the village next to the farm, and I was sure that it was now an estate. I drove down to the place and, sure enough, it was a large private housing estate about ten years old. I'd seen a map of the whole farm, and I decided to look at the houses that actually occupied the space where the haunted dwelling had once been.

I was somewhat surprised to find that this prime piece of the site, with trouble-free access to the village, was not developed, whereas further along in both directions the maximum number of houses possible had been placed. I used my press card to get some information from the builders who told me that there had been a lot of accidents associated with the project, and four men had lost their lives in an abortive attempt to bulldoze the building, and another two had been killed by falling masonry.

It was starting to sound familiar, and I asked how the building had eventually been demolished. The press officer, whom I had known from a previous job, looked a bit embarrassed and handed me an old cutting from the local paper. It told how a passing motorist had reported a black man, or a man in all-black clothes, of huge stature, climbing over the roof. When the police arrived, the house was ablaze from top to bottom, and it seemed not worth taking any risks to put it out. There were more injuries in clearing the site, and a man died during the laying of foundations for two new houses. The other men then flatly refused to work on that part of the estate any more, saying that it was cursed. The local union backed them, and the builders gave in gracefully, marking the site only with a small plaque commemorating those of their staff who had lost their lives.

This case is one of a very rare type, and there is little known on the subject. Sir Arthur Conan Doyle, in his wonderful book *The Land of Mist*, does dramatize a case with some similarities, based on the findings of Lord St

Audries in a haunted house in Torquay, Devon. In Alec's experience, no attempt was made to communicate with the spirit, but it was done in the St Audries case. (Imprecations and threats offered to ghosts do *not* count as 'communicating'.) There was some response to reason, and the offer of help, in the St Audries case, but that was clearly one of a human soul tied to the spot. What this was, we are not in a position to say. What is interesting is that the crucifix, so beloved of fiction-writers, was, as events turned out, actually worse than useless, since it provided the spirit with a handy weapon. Some would argue, of course, that Alec's lack of any real conviction was the true reason why it didn't work, and that a believer would have been protected. If that is true, it is the belief that is protecting, not the crucifix. But that is a theological argument, and not one of interest to us.

As with all such stories, the central question is always the same: where is the sense in it all? Why should a powerful entity wish to remain in a miserable old house for years, perhaps centuries, doing nothing but rattle the tiles and light up the windows. Not to know must not be confused with there not being a reason, but in most ghost stories no serious effort is made to think the thing through and try to draw a broader view of the whole of psychic experiences.

What is needed is a scientific approach to all reported sightings. Private money to fund a Chair of Psychic Studies at a university – a team on red alert to go to any sighting as quickly as possible and to question witnesses and examine evidence. A retired senior detective could have a watching brief, and all discoveries would be stored on a computer in the hope that a positive pattern shows up. At the moment we have nothing like this, yet haunting is a subject of universal interest. Survival after death affects every person on this planet equally, and I know there would be no shortage of funds.

Hardly a day passes without my being asked to investigate some event or the other, simply because I am known to be sympathetic to the ideas of those who believe in a spirit dimension to the world. How much more so would people respond to a sort of psychic FBI?

A Childless Spirit?

I could fill up ten books with stories of hauntings, as there is hardly a locality in the country that does not have some such story buried in its past. Unfortunately, though, most of this is hearsay or the usual unsubstantiated tale of strange knockings or similar effects. That is certainly not to say that these are not authentic reports, but it would take an army of assessors years to sift and watch for all the supposed evidence there is. Reluctantly, therefore, I was forced to do the very thing I least like doing – going for the spectacular cases, rather than slowly unravelling a complex history of supernatural happenings.

It is funny, but it seemed to me, as I heard all these different accounts, that every haunting was unique in its own way: that psychic occurrences were not like everyday events, with a common ground, but somehow tailored to the surroundings and even to the individuals who experienced them. This is, of course, a warning note, for we all want to believe in another world after this one, and for some of us the creaking of timbers as the house cools at night is enough. For others, the evidence has to be so cast-iron as to make it impossible for them ever to be convinced. The knack lies in having an open enough mind to be able to see the obviously genuine, without being so gullible as to be taken in by the patently false. I hope I have been able to tread that difficult path.

Ghosts are not the prerogative of old houses or sites where violent events have happened but are mostly found in the ordinary spot where you would least expect them to be. I found that a quite disproportionate number of council houses were haunted, for example, and this is very odd. What is really funny is that people have to wait a long time to get a property from a council, and they don't want to rock the boat. It is from such people that I found the most convincing evidence. If you complain about ghosts to the housing department, they may be sympathetic, but you will have put yourself back a long way on the list, if you are even considered again. Therefore if a family ups sticks because of psychic problems, they have put up with these things until they became unbearable, and that is a case worth investigating!

Such was the case with Mr and Mrs Wright of North London, who had been recently allocated a very nice modern house. They had a girl of three and a cat.

For the first few weeks everything seemed perfect. They had the general hullaballoo of house-warmings and the ordering of furniture, so they were not in a receptive frame of mind. On the other hand, perhaps whatever it was (is) was biding its time. The first intimation was when Mrs Wright was told by neighbours that her husband was seeing another woman. A young woman had been seen at windows and, on one occasion, sitting in the garden. The husband worked staggered shifts, and his wife worked every morning at the local supermarket, the child staying with a council-approved minder. This led to rows, but Mrs Wright recalls that she didn't really believe the stories. However, she did find herself getting progressively more tense and irritable as their stay at the house grew longer. She was at a loss to explain this to herself, as she had never felt happier or more secure on a fundamental level. Her husband agrees that there was a peculiar atmosphere in the house when he came home to it while his wife was out, but he put it down to his having new responsibilities to face.

The neighbours continued to report the presence of this woman, so one day Mrs Wright, pretending to go off to work as usual, went round the houses and entered the neighbour opposite's back door, where she was conducted to the prime watching-position of the front bedroom. From there she clearly saw a woman of about her own age (twenty-nine) moving about the house with perfect assurance. Her husband was due home in an hour, and she waited with grim determination to see the outcome of their being alone together. As she watched, her neighbour's phone rang and, without thinking, Mrs Wright took the phone when told the call was for her. When she put the phone to her ear, she was deafened by a woman's terrible shrieking, and repeated demands for 'her baby back'. The voice was the most awful thing she'd ever heard, but she guessed who it was and rushed out of the house to confront the woman and get to the bottom of the whole matter.

Mrs Wright opened the door and quickly found no one downstairs, so she went upstairs. She heard some sounds from her and her husband's room and went across the landing, shouting something which she no longer remembers. The next instant the door was opened from the inside with such force that one of its hinges broke, and a blur of white hurtled out, straight for her. It bowled her over, and her only memory is of a warm wetness that brushed all across the exposed parts of her body. Whatever it was, and she is sure it was no woman, flew down the stairs with a sort of whoosh. Thoroughly frightened, Mrs Wright staggered down after it but found no sign anywhere. The back door remained fastened, and the neighbour, whose eyes had never left the place, reported that nobody had come through the front. There was a moist smell to the air, but no other hint that there had ever been anyone else there.

The door was repaired, but the atmosphere worsened. The spirit, or whatever it was, seemed obsessed with them when they were alone, and with the child when she was with them. They would find her clothes laid out neatly on the bed, or the pram prepared for a journey.

In their own room much more horrible things were happening. Mr Wright would find men's underwear under his wife's pillow, but with just the tips peeping out so that he could see them as he pulled the covers to get into bed. Mrs Wright would find exotic lingerie crudely hidden in her husband's shirt drawer. Pornographic magazines for both sexes would be found hidden inside his *Autocar* or her *Best*, and so it went on. Their nerves were ragged with worry about the child. She now slept with them, and they took it in turns to stay awake watching over her. They confess that, if it hadn't been the house of their dreams, they would have been out of the place like a shot. The last straw came when Mrs Wright, having dozed during her turn of duty, awoke to see the woman bending over the sleeping little girl, her arm raised. Now more angry than terrified, she flew at the woman and once again encountered the wetness and the smell. Mr Wright awoke to see his wife grappling with what appeared to be a sheet, his child awake and screaming her heart out, and the room full of a foul stench. They left immediately for her mother's house and have never set foot in the place again. Neither knows any of their family who was involved with losing a child, although that means nothing. I have discreetly questioned the new tenants, and they have had no bother whatsoever, although their child is only four. Significantly perhaps, he is a boy.

It is a curious fact that I have been to twelve haunted council houses, mostly in London, and *all* the spirits have been unpleasant – not all as dreadful as the Wrights' apparition, but some quite close.

The extraordinary prevalence of flame with these obnoxious manifestations is an odd thing. One family were regularly tipped out of bed by a woman with flame coming out of her eyes (this was seen on one occasion by two visitors, one a clergyman, the other a social worker). In the end one of the children was admitted to a mental hospital, and the council rehoused the family in a better place. That the family waited until they were *in extremis* does prove my point that people will put up with almost anything rather than quit their homes.

The Wrights' house was almost new. The previous tenants had moved into their own house but had been perfectly happy in the council one. As a matter of routine I checked their birth records, and there was no suggestion of any irregularity, such as an abortion or a fostering that went wrong, causing deep distress that might have lingered. The ghost used a telephone, but these pages are full of instances in which spirits can manipulate the real world. It is a comforting myth that such visitors are capable simply of showing themselves.

Poltergeists

This German word, meaning 'noisy ghost', identifies one of the commonest forms of spirit. They are completely universal and timeless, and very curious.

Of recent years there has been much speculation that they were not spirits at all but manifestations of adolescent energy. Once again, we see the hand of misguided science at work. Many don't believe that the mind can perform what is known as telekinesis or psychokinesis – that is to say, that someone can use mind over matter. At the same time they can't bear a psychic element in anything, so they fall between the two stools. There is no scientific proof as yet that any serious effect on the material world can be performed by the mind. That is not to say that it can't, and I happen to think that it can, but until it is demonstrated one way or the other, we must give equal attention to both theories. Certainly, much poltergeist activity does take place in the vicinity of young people, particularly those in the twelve-to-eighteen age group. On the other hand, much doesn't, so a closer examination of the facts is required. What we may be seeing is the supposed ability of the physical mind to manipulate the exterior world, which could be interpreted as the result of an external (psychic) force operating, but there is no way to be sure. For the purposes of this book, I will report poltergeist activity only where no children were involved. That is not to say that this power might not extend over a longer range than the immediate home, but we must draw the line somewhere.

The Boltons are a good example to start with. They are childless by choice, both professional people with none of the usual worries, as far as one can tell. When they took the house they have at present, the couple who were leaving (whose children were all grown up and gone from home) told them that they had 'Brownies' at the bottom of the garden. This was half in jest, but the woman of the house explained that little jobs would be done for them, as though by some benign little creatures of the kind one read about in fairytales. The Boltons treated this as a mild eccentricity and thought no more about it.

Peculiar things did start to happen almost right away, however, and they were at a loss to account for them. Dishes would be washed while they were out at work, the washing-machine would be operated and the clothes transferred to the tumble-drier. At first Jenny Bolton was convinced that she must be doing these things herself and forgetting them, and she visited her doctor. He found her perfectly well and prescribed a course of mild tranquillizers. The odd events continued, however, and now began to involve Peter Bolton. He would find the garden shed tidied or his clothes put in the wash or hung up in the wardrobes. The couple did become slightly worried at this – the sense of having 'goblins', however well-meaning, making free with your house is a disquieting one.

One day Jenny lost her temper when some fruit had been picked and placed in a box under the sink; she admits that the good deeds were getting on her nerves, and she spoke rather rudely. The first thing to happen was that the box of fruit was up-ended, and the loose apples flung around the kitchen. At this she became terrified and ran out of the house. She went to a neighbour's without telling her the real reason for the visit. After some tea she went back home to find the whole place in chaos. Soap powder had been tipped all over the vegetables, taps had been turned on and plugs put in, furniture had been knocked over and jam rubbed into her Persian carpet. She tried to ring her husband at the office, only to find the telephone plug pulled out. She left the house once again to phone from a callbox.

When she explained the situation to Peter, he promised to drive straight home. She waited in a small restaurant, dallying over a coffee until she saw him approach. They went into the house together to find it perfectly in order. Jenny found this even more terrifying than the wreckage, as it cast a doubt in her mind, and she knew it would in Peter's, as to whether she was going insane. He remembers feeling slightly suspicious, wondering if his wife had not in fact being been doing all the things that had been attributed to the 'fairies'. To seem to take her perfectly seriously, he examined some of the vegetables – to his surprise (and relief) there were traces of washing-powder among the leaves of some of them, and he turned to apologize to Jenny for his doubts. As he explained his find, pandemonium broke out – windows were smashed, plates, saucers and cups flew around the house, lights came on and off, and nothing seemed to be safe. Under attack, they retreated to the front door to make their escape, only to be showered by bedclothes from upstairs windows.

Neighbours turned out to see what on earth was disturbing the sedate avenue, and the police were called. As soon as they arrived, everything became calm again. The police listened politely enough, but it was clear they thought this was yet another case of a tiff that had got out of hand and that it had nothing to do with the occult.

The house had now an air of malevolence and was in such a state that the Boltons spent the night at an hotel. They returned the following morning to find the house once again tidy. They had, however, both seen enough of what could be done by the thing and declined to be lulled into a false sense of security with Heaven-knows-what ultimate result. They both report that the house was like a bomb ready to go off and that the atmosphere was intolerable. They collected as many personal things as they dared, then left for good.

The present tenants tell me that odd nice things do seem to happen, such as the sudden smell of fresh lemons in the house, or windows being opened when the house grows stuffy during the day. Clearly the spirit has learnt that small is beautiful, as far as most people are concerned, and has moderated its efforts accordingly.

All cultures have a name for this helpful sprite, but this is the best evidence I have heard for the two sides there are to these mysterious beings.

I have been to see the ruins of the old caravan that was the scene of awful manifestations during the middle 1950s. It had been bought by Jim and Susan Barker and was sited about a half-mile from Susan's father's farm on a small piece of land acquired long before. It was linked to the farm by a lane and was in the most beautiful possible position, with panoramic views of the surrounding countryside. It was a strange contrast, this idyllic setting and the dreadful sights and sounds that were to take place there.

The vehicle was brand new and very luxuriously appointed. Electric power was laid on, and every modern convenience had been installed. Jim had a job in a nearby town, and Susan would do part-time work in the office of the farm. They planned to cultivate much of the acre and a half that comprised the site, and to become partly self-sufficient.

Perhaps a clue to the mystery is visible in some aerial photos taken of the farm by people who were searching for an old Roman encampment and hoped to find its unmistakable outline from above. They were unsuccessful but gave the farmer the pictures as a keepsake and moved on. What these show is the outline of another road that meets the lane at the caravan site. When the village it served was demolished to make way for a new reservoir, it had soon reverted to farmland. Nevertheless, its outline is very clear from the pictures. As it was at crossroads that suicides were buried and criminals hung in cages, there were obviously bad connections with the place, although no one thought about that at the time. (As an aside, readers may be interested to know that before suicide ceased to be a crime in the 1960s, the verdict on a suicide case was traditionally '… took his own life while the balance of the mind was disturbed'. This form of words allowed the loathsome practice of burying people in unhallowed ground to be circumvented.)

The first signs that something was amiss came with the sound of a bellowing voice awaking the Barkers again and again in the small hours. Despite Susan's father's turning out with a watch of men, the perpetrator was never discovered. The noise subsided for a little while, to be replaced by muck from the farm being tipped into the caravan, culminating in the couple's waking up soaking wet one morning to find that the whole of the bed had been covered with the contents of a local cess-pit. This revolting episode forced them to take temporary accommodation at the farm while the caravan was cleaned and disinfected.

The local police launched a full-scale hunt for a lunatic with a grudge against the family. Many were questioned, but there was no evidence against anyone.

The farmer was a rich man, often reason enough in itself, but he was also respected by all members of the community, and there is little doubt that the malefactor would have been known to the village people if he were one of them, and handed over to the authorities. He was also a magistrate, however, and thus there may have been many people – living and dead – who harboured grudges against him.

Their home now being as good as new, the young couple moved back. This time, however, a covert watch was kept on the premises by the father and a rota of his employees. Nobody begrudged the time on guard, for everyone had known Susan since she was a young girl, and her husband was a popular member of many village activities.

As he was preparing for bed that night, Jim was alarmed by a scream from his wife, who was in the living-room. Pouring down from where the wall joined the roof was a long stream of blood (later identified as pigs' blood) which soaked the carpet. The scream had also alerted the guard, and he and Jim circled the caravan time and again, looking for some hidden person or device, but none could be found. Yet still the stream continued to pour down the wall. Once again they evacuated the caravan for it to be cleaned, and the police redoubled their efforts. There can be no doubt that the investigation was of the utmost stringency as Susan's father was, as I have remarked, a highly respected man. Despite every effort by forensic scientists, no clue could be found, and then the supernatural was suspected. That over ten gallons of blood could be tipped down between two tightly fitting pieces of wood and metal, while two men searched below with torches, seemed to defy all normal explanation.

At this stage a TV set was purchased by the farmer,

together with one for the caravan – as a sort of consolation, perhaps. The guard was now mounted by one of the farm labourers and a special constable; discreet lights were placed at positions of vantage so that the whole of the caravan was under constant observation. Extra-thick curtains were fitted, and the couple prepared for another try at living in what had originally been their dream home.

Neither admits that they placed much credence in the supernatural theory, rather preferring the idea of a very ingenious enemy with a grudge – either that or a lunatic, although that seemed the unlikeliest explanation of all. With this idea uppermost, they felt quite secure in the cosy warmth of their living-room, with men and dogs on patrol at all times. It was, they recall, not the ideal situation for a newly married couple, but if it deterred the pest, they were quite prepared to make such a comparatively small sacrifice.

They switched on the new TV, much excited by the novelty. The programme seemed normal enough for a few minutes, then the picture began to flicker. They had been warned that TV pictures in this location were not as reliable as those nearer the transmitter, and that TV as a whole was still coming to terms with the new technology. The picture, when it returned to normal, was of a large, yawning hole, rather like some local caves; then there was a low chuckle of great menace, and a hideous snarling face appeared on the screen. Jim complained that he thought it usual for some warning to be given if frightening material was to be shown, and the TV shouted back, 'This is a warning – I'm going to kill you both – like this.' As they watched in terror, they saw their own faces on the screen being smashed to pieces by sledge-hammers.

The set began to bellow just as the original nuisance had, and there came an urgent knocking at the door. They found it difficult to take their eyes from the screen as they saw human organs ripped to pieces in front of them, all to the accompaniment of the insane bellowing. The two guards forced the door and dragged the terrified pair into the open as flames began to pour from the TV.

Within minutes the caravan was a gutted wreck, and

one of the most horrific incidents of poltergeist activity on record had come to an end.

The Woman who 'Caught' Coincidences

This story is unique, not only in itself but because it raises profound questions about the nature of the universe in a way quite different from those raised in the other stories. With *them*, we do at least have some sort of answer, however improbable; *this* is outside all normal understanding. The superficial view, that everything that happened was the result of random chance, is unsatisfactory. For a start, there seems to be an element of what we humans would call 'devilment'. It smacks of a prank by some superior force – this force went slightly too far and nearly caused a nervous breakdown, but the things themselves were harmless enough, and no intention to hurt can be discovered. However, if this is the explanation, it is a disquieting one. That creatures with such power can act irresponsibly is a frightening thought. It must be said that chance *could* have produced the effects, but read the story and see if you think, as I do, that some sort of *positive* agency must have been at work.

Winifred and Lawrence Hazlitt went south in the middle 1930s, looking for something better than their depressed county of Lancashire in which to bring up their hoped-for family. They settled in the mushrooming suburbs of Croydon, near the town of Sutton, in Surrey. This was the area of Henry VIII's palace at Nonsuch, Wimbledon tennis was just down the road, and the King and Queen drove through their streets every year on the way to the Derby, a few miles further on into the South Downs. There was prosperity here, and hope for the future; above all, there were jobs, and Lawrence had no difficulty in finding an outlet for his engineering talents.

Their family was still very young when the war came, but they survived it without loss of limb or property, then once again the couple looked forward to raising the children in peace and comfort. By the late 1950s both the boys had married, and Winifred had the chance to devote herself to long-neglected interests. She attended, and hosted, card parties (they were the last great days of the whist-drive), concerned herself with social work in a small way and generally exploited her new-found freedom by reading widely and visiting the numerous places of interest in and around London. She was more than contented and visualized for herself nothing more than serious pleasures, tempered by putting something back into the community in return for all the benefits she and her family had received from it. Her world was safe and ordered, and she could imagine nothing that could disturb it.

In the spring of 1958, she recalls, she was preparing dinner at home when an unusual sound caught her attention, coming from the living-room. It sounded like sausages cooking and, fearing a fire, she went quickly in. The noise was louder there, but it seemed to be coming from all around. Very worried, she began to pull out pieces of furniture and examined the electrical connections. Then she became aware of a strange light that had formed itself in the French windows. She describes it as white with a dash of orange – peach, but not peach. This, like the hissing, was growing in intensity. She suddenly felt faint and unsteady on her feet, and the room took on the look of something seen in the three mirrors of a dressing-table: everything seemed to be multiplying itself into infinity. From out of this kaleidoscope of images came rushing, as if making for her, two huge numbers, both ones, making a gigantic eleven, the number of her house. She passed out.

Fortunately Lawrence arrived home early and sent for an ambulance. He neither saw nor heard anything unusual.

Winifred was taken to St Helier hospital, at that time the largest in Europe, where she remained unconscious until the evening of the next day. She awoke ravenously hungry and declaring that she had never felt better. With difficulty, she was persuaded to stay until the following morning, when the duty doctor could decide whether she was well enough to leave. She ate a substantial meal, read a book and slept like a top.

In the morning she was anxious to get home and paid scant attention to what she considered to be the doctor's small-talk. He remarked that Hazlitt was his wife's maiden name and that they had the same birthday; one thing led to another, and she discovered that his name was Lawrence, too, and that he was the same age as her husband. It interested her slightly, but the thought of getting out was occupying almost all her thoughts. As for the cause of the trouble in the first place, it was the doctor's opinion that she had been overworking. This is always a palatable diagnosis, as we all secretly believe it to be a condition we suffer from, and Winifred was no exception. With this flattering explanation behind her, she was more than ready to accept the cure – a good long holiday, with plenty of fresh fruit and vegetables; the general sort of good advice a doctor might give anybody.

A taxi had been summoned, a luxury she rarely permitted herself, and she was feeling very cheerful as she made her way to the car-park. When she got to it, she found, to her total amazement, that the driver was an old schoolfriend whom she had not seen for almost thirty years. They were both flabbergasted and soon exchanging details of their present lives. Winifred's friend had moved south shortly after she had, and now lived in the borough next to hers at, he said, 11 Rochester Avenue. It was astonishing: she lived at 11 Rochester Road in her own borough. He had two sons, both married and both the same age as hers, and his wife was also a Winifred. She recalls a slight feeling of unease overtaking her, but it faded as she made arrangements for a reunion as soon as she returned from her holiday.

She went into the house, unaware that she had just taken part in the opening stages of a drama that would threaten her sanity before the day was out, although no incident was in itself fantastic or horrifying, and in normal circumstances each could be shrugged off with a wondering shake of the head.

Her husband had had urgent business and could neither collect nor meet her, and for this she was strangely glad, as the calm and solitude of their beautiful home seemed to be what she needed. It being Thursday, she decided to call her friend Anne, to see whether the usual whist party was on for that night. She lifted the receiver and was startled to hear Anne's voice. At the time, Winifred believed that Anne had dialled her number while thinking she was calling someone else, but in the light of subsequent events she now thinks that Anne's explanation – that it was the remarkable coincidence of getting as a wrong number a person who is on the point of calling you – might well be correct. They chatted for a little while and confirmed the time for the evening game.

Winifred then decided to call her husband, to let him know all was well and that she had a clean bill of health from the hospital. She was also rather anxious to give him the maximum time to accept the idea of the holiday. She dialled and was put through, and they had a long conversation. She heard that their sons had called regularly for bulletins, their homes in Northumberland and Wales making it impossible for them to visit at such short notice.

After about ten minutes, he asked, 'Whose phone are you using?' Surprised, she said, 'Ours, of course.' There was a long silence.

Then he said, 'Am I speaking to Mrs Winifred Potter?'

She remembers the shock she felt. The timbre of his voice seemed suddenly different, and odd inconsistencies which she had put down to the poor line came flooding back. She had been talking to a stranger for almost a quarter of an hour, but a stranger whose life, voice and experiences (even to having a wife with the same name who was due out of hospital at the same time) were almost identical to her own husband's. Obviously they were a household without a phone, not uncommon in the late fifties, and had it not been for that, the astonishing fact might not have come out. She panicked, she recalls with shame, and slammed the phone down. Feeling shaky, she decided it must be due partly to her having eaten only two meals in seventy-two hours.

Winifred went into the kitchen to make herself a sandwich and some coffee before phoning her real husband. The thought made her smile, but that soon disappeared when she found no coffee or bread in the house. It was a ten-minute hike to the shops, but she knew she couldn't last the day without something, so she reluctantly put on her coat.

On the doorstep, as though left by a benign Providence,

was a box of groceries, including coffee and bread. She took back the reproaches she had heaped on her husband's head and made herself an ample snack. Only later, when she looked at the bill, did she realize that it had been delivered to the wrong house. It should have gone to 111. She blessed the carelessness of the delivery boy and made a note to order a duplicate and have it sent to the proper address.

She was having a third cup of coffee when the doorbell rang with the parcel post. It brought her a package from the mail-order firm she used for odd items of clothing and household goods. As she knelt to cut the wrappings, an envelope top caught her eye, poking out from one of the folds in the brown paper. She took it out, intending to give it to the postman in the morning, when her startled eyes fell on the address. It was to a Mrs Bolton of 11 Canal Street in her home town and, what was even more incredible, it was in her mother's handwriting. She herself knew the Boltons well. An eerie feeling swept over her, and she became irrationally afraid. Of all the millions of letters that could have been trapped, it had to be one from her own mother, and addressed to a house with the number 11.

Winifred recovered herself quickly enough when the telephone rang. It was Lawrence, enquiring after her, and she felt considerable reassurance in listening to his strong voice. She told him about the holiday and was relieved to find him in total agreement with the doctor. Then she told him about the card game that night.

'That's good,' he answered, 'only I met a chap on the train this morning – haven't seen him since college, and he wanted me to have a pint on the way home. I was just going to have a quick one, but if you're going out, we can have a bite to eat as well and talk over old times. I may have mentioned him. Bit of a coincidence actually: he's a Lawrence, married to a Winifred, too.'

She blurted out, 'Lawrence Potter?' and he chuckled, 'I was sure I must have said something – good, you have a nice time, and I'll have the kettle on when you get back. Bye.'

She put the phone down, rather weakly, a sensation

almost of claustrophobia coming over her. Everything seemed to be interconnected in the oddest way, and she felt faintly sick. That she had got a wrong connection to the very man her husband had met that morning, with all the similarities involved, seemed very strange and frightening. She decided to have a lie down; after all, the doctor had recommended as much rest as possible. Strangely, despite everything, she fell asleep almost immediately, awakening when the alarm rang at four, feeling immensely better and ashamed of her reaction to a few odd coincidences.

She remembered to telephone the grocer and was happy to brush aside his apologies, remarking on what a stroke of good fortune it had been. The grocer knew everyone's business and acted as a clearing-house for information, whether you wanted it or not. He volunteered the fact that the people in 111 were the Harts, husband, wife, four children and two grandparents, and that they were staying only until their new house was built.

At a quarter past seven Winifred set out for Anne's house, thinking that a few hours of whist and a chat would make her feel back in the swim of things. There were three people standing at her friend's door, talking to her, and all were looking mystified.

'Winnie, can you help? These people are sure that there's a family called Hart in the street, but I've never heard of them.'

With her knowledge from the grocer, she was able to put them right. As the woman was going, she turned to thank her. 'My name's Win, too; that's my husband, Lawrence, and my brother, Jack.' She shook hands, then they walked off down the road.

Winifred says she remembers feeling very little at this further example of chance; perhaps she had become numb by over-exposure. She didn't know it but, although these weird happenings were about to come to an end, they intended to go out in a blaze of glory.

There was a cheerful fire, and friendly faces, and she relaxed properly for the first time that day. They were all good players, and their evenings were usually very enjoyable; tonight, however, was destined to be remarkable rather than pleasant.

'I actually felt like vomiting when I picked up the first hand,' she says. 'There were eleven hearts in it, starting at the ace and finishing with the jack; it was the total number of people called Hart whom I had encountered in one way or the other that day, and the last was a Jack.'

Somehow she kept calm, for the sake of the others, but when the next hand was identical, she burst into terrified tears. Thinking that this was a continuation of her earlier illness, her friends got her into a chair, and brandy and a cigarette were produced. Under their calming influence, she started to try to explain what had been happening. At that moment, the youngest son of the house came in, from football practice. On his white shirt there was a red heart with the number 11 on it. Winifred let out a horrified scream, and the poor child fled upstairs, while the two Alsatians that had been sitting contentedly by the fire began to bark. To add to the pandemonium, there was a ring at the doorbell, 'Who is it?' shouted the hostess, her nerves on edge.

'Butcher's boy. Mr Smith says he can't give you your usual three, so he's sent all he has of the small ones.'

Forgetting, in her excited state, that it was her regular order for the dogs, she shouted back, 'What are you talking about?' and received the answer, 'Eleven small ones – eleven hearts.'

At this Winifred became so distressed that the doctor was called, and he sent her back to hospital. From there she was transferred to what was called a private sanatorium – a euphemism for a lunatic asylum. There, with gentle care and a cessation of the coincidence plague, she rapidly recovered, and she was soon able to go on holiday with her husband.

Apart from the run-of-the-mill curiosities that happen to us all, the weird phenomenon has not returned.

It may be significant that the trouble was first noticed at about nine in the morning and came to an end at about eight at night – a period of eleven hours. On the other hand, it may just be a coincidence!

Meetings – A Miscellany II

The phrase 'You look as if you've seen a ghost!' is a very misleading one. In 'Doctor in the House', there is no real fear of the apparition, although the spirit in 'A Terrifying Phantom' *is* terrifying. But he isn't terrifying *because* he is a ghost, only by the nature of his ghostliness. He would be terrifying even as a living human being!

My real reason for saying that the phrase is misleading, however, is because a lot of meetings with ghosts aren't recognized as such. My research indicates that we have all met them at one time or another; it is only later, when some inconsistency or special knowledge comes our way, that we suspect the true nature of the encounter. Human history is littered with tales of ghosts, but rarely are they of the shrieking banshee type so beloved of the Gothic novel. In all cultures people have seen ghosts, and these have often come as warnings of dangers to the person who saw them, so a benign element is very strong in almost all stories worth a moment's examination. When Brutus sees the ghost of the murdered Caesar, of course, that is very likely an evil conscience and a justifiable fear of what will happen to him at the hands of Mark Antony at the Battle of Philippi. Such convenient ghosts should not delay us in our search for the true nature of spirits, mainly because they are not evidential – that is to say, they do not bring a message that the observer could not be expected to know already. To put it crudely, we are looking for the sort of manifestation which says, 'The 3.30 express will be derailed at Norwich' while it is still only two o'clock. The evidence does not necessarily have to be as dramatic as that, but the essence of the idea must be there. The second class of this kind of thing is where the ghost has about it something particularly out of order for its time. Here, too – though it is preferable to have two or more witnesses – I have included a couple that do not fall into that category.

Mrs Jones, late of Tower Hamlets, a poor borough of East London, has, since the incident I am about to describe, married into a higher level of society. Consequently she wishes as little background detail about herself as possible to appear in print. However, I have also spoken to her daughter (now a married woman herself), and the facts seem strong enough to count as a genuine encounter with a spirit.

It was during the great heatwave of 1976 that Susan (the daughter) came indoors to ask if a new friend, a girl called Jane, could come in for some tea. They had been playing in the street for about an hour and were both very hot. Mrs Jones was very preoccupied, said yes and got on with her work. She heard the children laughing in the kitchen, and the sound of bottles and jars being opened. She remembers well, despite her own concerns, the constant squeals of excitement and wonder the girl Jane was making. Even making allowances for the run-down district, the child's appreciation seemed somewhat excessive. (Run-down physically much of East London is, but that implies no criticism of the people themselves, who are a generous and honest group of people.) When she heard the girl ask if this was the Queen's house, her suspicions were aroused.

Going into the kitchen, she was horrified to see her daughter's companion. She was small for her age, which seemed much as Susan's, Mrs Jones later recalled, and she was indescribably dirty. As she got closer, she saw that the child's dress, although superficially no grubbier than her own daughter's after an hour's playing in the streets, was inherently filthy. It had obviously been washed recently, but it was uniformly grey, as though it had only been sluiced out in water without soap, let alone washing-powder. That was bad enough, but the girl was obviously suffering from every sort of vermin. Her skin was peppered in flea-bites, her hair crawling with lice that Mrs

Jones was mercifully unfamiliar with. The girl had no eyes
for her, however, but kept picking up ordinary household
items and fondling them with unalloyed admiration and
wonder.

Mrs Jones' sympathies were all with the little girl, and
she decided to give Jane a bath and call the police.
Masking her horror, she asked the girls if they would like a
bath, receiving the reply from Jane, 'What's a bath?'
Reassuring the girl that it was something nice, she pulled
off her lousy clothes and the red cloth band in her hair and
ordered Susan to run the bath. She cut the girl a huge
chunk of bread, with a liberal spread of jam (she looking
very under-nourished) and threw the offending clothes
into a bucket and poured copious quantities of Dettol over
them. Their guest revelled in what was probably her first
bath, once again picking up first one thing, then another,
always with gurgles of excitement. Her hair was
shampooed and cream rubbed onto the myriad little bites.
Finally, when Jane was adorned in one of Susan's dresses,
the children sat down to more food and to play with dolls
(another novelty).

There was nothing Mrs Jones detested more than
neglect of children, yet she had to admit that the child
showed no signs of abuse, and her being touched by a
strange adult had not produced any sign of fear. She
realized that the child's home background must be put
right, but she was loath to take the ultimate and
irreversible step of alerting the police. She examined the
discarded clothes for any name-tags that might be sewn
on but found nothing. The dress went into the dustbin,
but the headband she kept – she felt it might have some
sentimental value to the girl or her family.

Mrs Jones knew that social workers visited some local
families, so she determined to speak to one of them first
and to be guided accordingly. She was just putting on her
coat when Susan appeared to ask where Jane had gone.
Susan had gone to the toilet, only to find her missing
when she returned. They searched the flat and the stairs
of the block, but with no success. Then the police were
called, but likewise found nothing. No very serious view
was taken of the matter – a poor little girl had had a nice

afternoon out, got a new dress and decided to go home. It was impossible to convey to them the thoroughly wretched state of the child, and the best the police could reasonably promise to do was to check their files of missing children and tell the neighbourhood policemen to keep their eyes open.

Jane was never seen again, although, if the authorities' idea was the correct one, she would surely have come back often to what she obviously regarded as a cornucopia. The headband was kept, against Jane's making a return in search of it. It was put away at the back of a drawer and when the family moved, they took it with them. An antique-clothing expert put it as cheapjack Victorian, not later than 1860–70, so one must assume 'the Queen's house' asked about was not our present monarch's.

One cannot help wondering what strange story little Jane must have told her anxious parents when she returned clean, in lovely clothes and with a mass of memories that would make no sense to anybody.

The next story is a rare exception in these cases, because it involves only one person. However, the narrator is so convincing and capable that I can't find fault with his narrative. Likewise, the story does him no credit, and that is a good guide. For a professional army officer to admit to having had a long conversation with a ghost (?) takes a lot of courage and is certainly something I should have thought twice about when I was in the Services.

It was at the end of some routine exercise on Salisbury Plain on July 9 that the lieutenant came to lose the rest of the small party he was with. It was a bright afternoon, and he had paused (momentarily – he thought) to adjust some equipment that was causing him irritation. Whether he took longer than he thought and the rest were genuinely out of sight, we can't establish. There have been theories (and 'The Armada Ship' is an example) that two times may come together as one, their inhabitants co-existing, neither being a 'ghost' because neither has been through the process of dying at the time of the meeting. The lieutenant recalls feeling nothing more than annoyance with himself

– he had a compass and was very experienced in making his way safely over terrain much worse than this.

After a few minutes he saw a figure approaching. When it came close enough for physical details to be discerned, he saw it was a man carrying a gun and looking very dishevelled. At the sight of the lieutenant ('John' from hereon), he backed away, bringing his gun to the firing position. This was extremely ominous, to put it mildly, and John raised his arms and waved them from side to side in what he hoped was a gesture dismissing any threat. He also loosed the band holding his own gun and lowered it carefully to the ground, walking away as he did so but with the added purpose of allowing him to get his revolver out unseen. He then sat down and cheerily waved the other man over to join him. This he did, rather gingerly, and as he got really close, John could see that he was in a bad way indeed, almost dead on his feet. What he was wasn't immediately visible, but the first impression – of a rural homicidal maniac – was passing off.

The man spent a few seconds examining John, then clearly made up his mind to take a chance and wearily sat down beside him. The first thing John was conscious of was a sweetish smell, then considerable dirt on what had once been some sort of linen shirt and leather trousers. The gun was what caught his eye most, being a very ancient weapon of great size and weight, and clearly of the old gunpowder, not cartridge, operation. A ramrod was visible, and an ammunition pouch and what could have been a powder horn. The man was either lost from the set of an historical film or an eccentric lover of old firearms. To John's professional eye, however, the gun, for all its antiquity, looked as if it worked.

He handed the man his water-bottle, and the other drank thirstily, thanking him in a broad West Country accent. John still had plenty of food, and he proffered it, having it accepted in the same grateful fashion. When the man was refreshed, John asked him about himself, and the man became angry. He asked John if he was for the Duke, and John – thinking he was going along with a heavy-handed joke – replied that he was for the Queen. This was clearly the wrong answer, for the man tried to jump up and bring his gun into play. Gravely disturbed, John was forced to hit and disarm him. The man appeared to collapse, morally more than physically, and John questioned him further. During the next hour or so the man, who did not appear to be overburdened with intelligence, told him that he had been a soldier for the Duke of Monmouth, whose army had been wiped out near Sedgemoor. It was really odd, John told me, but I had no doubt that the fellow was telling the truth. If he had told me he was an eccentric millionaire who did this for fun, I don't think I'd have believed him, but I felt that what he was saying was the truth. If it was, John was in trouble: a seventeenth-century soldier would be the toast of the twentieth-century world, but the reverse could not be relied upon.

John also remembers (and this is a curious impression received by most people in these situations) a sort of tension in the air. It was like being near a large hidden generator, to use his phrase, and he was filled with the idea that this was making these strange events happen and if he could escape its influence he would get back to his own world. He quickly picked up the old fowling-piece, or whatever it was, fired it and threw the ramrod down the hill where it would still be visible but out of immediate reach. He then gave the open-mouthed soldier the balance of his food and his water-bottle, picked up his own gun and prepared to leave. He shook the man's hand and wished him good luck, then doubled away in the opposite direction, grasping his pistol. He turned twice to see the man staring after him. The third time there was no sign, and within an hour he was back with his own army.

John says he was tempted to take the man's gun to test the validity of what he believed but, as one soldier to another, to leave him defenceless would have been unthinkable. All he can produce, rather shamefacedly, is a receipt for a new water-bottle dated 12 July, but that is enough for me.

The next encounter is not a pleasant one, although there is a sort of happy ending. These strange events occurred in the autumn of 1983 in a medium-sized Berkshire town.

The house that was the epicentre of the troubles was a very old one, some parts of it thought to be eighteenth-century, and these manifestations had been going on for years. Like many places of a forbidding nature, it had always had a bad name, but, unlike the generality of such places, it did indeed seem to exert a malign influence over the neighbourhood and does have parallels with 'A Terrible Phantom', although there can be no doubt of a human cause to this one.

For many years the place had lain empty, with only an occasional event disturbing the surrounding area. Nonetheless, when these did happen, they were of a very violent nature. A district nurse taking a short-cut home past the place was knocked from her bicycle and kicked very hard. It was only early evening and was witnessed by two ladies who agree with the nurse that no physical assailant was visible. This was added to a long list of similar incidents and stored up in the folklore of the place. Then, out of the blue, the house was sold to a young couple who were as impressed by its potential for development into a very desirable residence as they were unimpressed by its history and reputation. They were soon to be disabused of this attitude, and a long series of misfortunes befell them.

Workmen were injured, plaster fell down with no good reason, small fires were discovered and, worst of all, some sort of force was starting to make itself visible with greater clarity and frequency. It showed itself at night mostly, but there were also daytime sightings, and it appeared to be the form of a small man, much bent. This, as we have seen in other stories, would not in itself be too dreadful, but the spirit would suddenly appear in the worst-lit parts of the house without warning, making hideous hissing noises. Something also took to scratching at doors at all times of the day and night and, hard-headed as the new occupants were, this began to unsettle them.

Then it learnt how to extinguish lights, and that became too much. To have a room plunged into darkness, then to hear the furtive scrabblings of the evil old spirit, became too much even for the doughty inhabitants. Far from wishing to drive them away, however, its new tactics seemed bent on keeping them in. As they reluctantly packed, it threw their clothes back into the wardrobes and drawers, and the tyres of their car were let down. This had a curious effect: they had started out defiant, they had become scared, now they reverted to defiance again. They steeled their nerves and called in one of the most prominent exorcists they could find. He was a clergyman with a formidable reputation for fearlessness and skill.

On the night set for the exorcism, the house was pandemonium. The spirit either feared or resented the coming ceremony, and noises came from all parts of the house. The exorcist used no formal procedures, preferring to confront the spirit head-on in the hope of helping; only if all else failed would any attempt be made to try to banish it. Present at the scene were the exorcist himself, his wife (who acted as his assistant) and the two householders. Also, of course, the unquiet soul for whose benefit the whole drama was being staged.

The meeting began with a prayer for the relief of the tormented ghost and to call down the help of God and good spirits to assist in what the exorcist called 'the process of curing'. The prayer was only half over when the lights went out, but this had been anticipated and torches were produced. The immediate result of this was to drive the spirit into a brief but terrible orgy of destruction. The torch was ripped from the exorcist's hand and flung with terrific force at his wife, striking her hard enough on the shoulder to knock her from her chair. The owners had been thoroughly briefed not to respond to any action unless the victim or the exorcist called for assistance. The torch did not go out and, perhaps feeling thwarted, the spirit began to switch the main lights on and off with bewildering speed, which caused them to fuse.

Once again they turned their torches to the end of the room which seemed to be source of the power, the bright beams silhouetting an object that was forming against the curtained French windows. From this mass there came a wind that howled and screamed through the room. This was soon accompanied by little flecks of ice that struck like bullets. The two owners remember falling to their knees, babbling almost-forgotten prayers, as the thing began a slow advance down the length of the room towards the exorcist and his wife, who stood their ground against this awful and threatening presence. In a voice that bellowed to be heard above the hellish din the exorcist offered no reproach but continued his supplications to a higher power, and his pleas to the hideous monstrosity that was almost upon them.

Then the dreadful noises stopped, as did the moving mass. There was a dim radiance in the room now, and a feeling of peace permeated. The couple who had been, only moments before, semi-conscious with terror and revulsion, felt the calm pour out from the exorcist as he advanced the few paces to meet the now quiescent demon. With his wife by his side, he knelt with the thing, and the low murmur of voices could be heard in question and answer. Slowly the dark blob began to change into the kneeling figure of the old man who had caused so much fear and trouble, and then to disappear altogether.

'He took advantage of the good people who came,' the exorcist explained later, 'and he will go on to face whatever punishment awaits, because undetected murder was done here long ago – savage and cold-blooded murder.' He paused to accept hot coffee. 'But he has suffered a lot here, and that will count in his favour. He was like a young boy who knows he's done something bad and goes the wrong way about getting sympathy and forgiveness. That's what he's wanted and needed for very many years, and tonight it came to him, although he nearly didn't recognize it, which is why exorcism must be about help, not rejection. I think that spiritual energy builds up the longer a soul lives without redemption, and that that energy can kill people on earth. I had no idea it was so powerful, I've put everyone at risk, and I'm sorry.'

The house is now a warm and comfortable dwelling and there is a very peaceful atmosphere, something almost spiritual, about the place.

This report I received from the couple who own the house, but I have met the clergyman-exorcist (on an entirely different matter), and he assures me there are some cases in which people have been killed by rash attempts at exorcism. For an example of the power of spirits (even well-disposed ones) to flout and deride the power of priests, readers should recall 'A Well-meaning Spirit'.

UFOs

The Flying (Saucer) Doctors

I don't think there are many rational people left who think that Unidentified Flying Objects (UFOs) don't exist. This is due partly to the dropping of the term 'flying saucer', and partly to a greater awareness of the nature of the universe. The latter attitude is almost entirely the result of the TV documentary. The greatest single factor, however, must have been the American space programme. Year in and year out, we watched tremendous achievements in technology taking place, literally, in front of our very eyes. Live TV of the Moon-landing, pictures of men walking around in space, views of Mars and the distant planets from unmanned probes: all created the atmosphere in which people realized that, if mankind can go travelling to other worlds, why not the reverse? By the 1970s this Western *glasnost* has reached the point at which the governor of Georgia, later President Carter, could twice report seeing UFOs without jeopardizing his political hopes. The Duke of Edinburgh is on record as saying that he believes in UFOs.

Nevertheless, although belief in these things is widespread, actually saying that you've seen one is another matter. It is as though people say to themselves; 'I'm a reasonable person, but other people are not.' Consequently, the number of phenomena that gets reported is still minimal, with some honourable exceptions.

The experience of David and Margaret Brennan is unusual by any standards, but that is only in comparison with other reports. I am convinced that face-to-face encounters with extra-terrestrials are going on all the time, but either people do not realize the enormity of what has happened or the enormity convinces them that silence is the most

93

prudent course. Certainly, the Brennans made no effort to tell anyone but some close friends and, in fact, were at pains to extract promises of confidentiality even from them. It was from one of these 'confidential' sources that I first heard the story, a cautionary tale in itself, but I was able to convince David and Margaret that a greater good might be served if they let me give their experience a wider audience and that I, unlike their friends, would under no circumstances reveal their true identity.

The Brennans arranged to spend the Christmas holiday of 1987 with friends in one of the picturesque villages of Cornwall. The day for their departure was brilliantly sunny and warm, and they made good progress as far as Somerset, where a bad snarl-up kept them waiting for more than two hours. It was now nearly nine, and they were ravenously hungry, so they stopped at a transport café for dinner. They freely admit that, at the time, Brian, still not fully qualified as an accountant, and Margaret, a nurse, had little spare cash after paying the mortgage and the 101 other things that go with it. They would have liked to have stayed in an hotel, but that would have used up all their holiday money, so they decided to push on. They reached Exeter at about half-past ten and stopped to consult their map. Callington was the nearest big town to their destination, and this left them in a quandary: they could either take the A30 to Launceston, then drive down, or go via Plymouth and drive up. By that time Brian was feeling the strain of having been driving all day and suggested that, if they took the B3212 across Dartmoor to Tavistock, they would halve the distance and probably avoid the congestion of the A-roads. Margaret agreed, and they set off gaily, thinking themselves very clever to have found a route better than the one recommended by their more experienced hosts. Brian admitted he thought Dartmoor was no different from the rest of Devon, but simply a place where people kept sheep and ponies, instead of farming.

The weather had slowly deteriorated from late afternoon, and now a fairly strong gale was blowing and flecks of melting snow began to appear on the windscreen. It began to get very cold, and the snow turned to tiny particles of ice, lashing the windows under the full force of the wind. The heater, never much good, seemed to have given up the struggle, and the condensation began to freeze on the inside of the windows. There had been no other traffic visible for a long time, and Margaret became slightly alarmed, but she said nothing. They had been incredibly imprudent in their packing, she recalls. In their minds' eye they had called up those famous pictures of St Ives, with palm trees and exotic flowers growing in the depths of winter and, recalling the common expression 'the Cornish Riviera', had imagined they were going to some sort of British Florida. As a consequence, they had no warm clothing, no emergency heating, no brandy or even hot coffee.

The incidents after that they will never forget. Brian stopped the car, and his teeth were almost chattering.

'I don't like this at all, love. We've got to get somewhere warm, and fast. My hands and feet are getting numb, and it's hard to drive. I'm turning back. Keep your eyes peeled for a farmhouse or something.'

The tone of his voice terrified Margaret, and she stared out of the window, hoping to see a glimmer of light through the swirling snow and sleet. Brian turned the car, and they headed back towards Exeter. Then she did see a light, a momentary gleam to their right. 'Turn right!' she screamed. She remembers that the sight of safety crystallized all her terrors and made it seem as if it were their only hope. Brian swung the car onto the narrow track picked out in the headlamps, misjudged his angle and sent the car spinning off the road into a ditch. As he revved the motor to escape, the wheels dug themselves deeper into the wet ground. They got out to look and, with the help of a small torch, saw the hopelessness of the situation. The car was buried up to its axle in mud, and it would need a tractor to get it out. The coldness of the wind was unbelievable, coming in unchecked from the sea and carrying a sandy sleet that stung savagely.

'Where was the light?' Brian shouted. Margaret pointed down the lane, but there was nothing now to be seen. He threw open the boot, and they ransacked it for every item of clothing there was, which was precious little. A couple of thin sweaters each, and two anoraks. They struggled into this inadequate protection, then Brian switched off the engine and lights. Supporting each other around the shoulders, they set off towards the light that Margaret had seen. The ground was sloshy and made walking even more arduous than it might normally have been. It was only later, when they compared notes, that they found that they were both surprised how much they could endure. Certainly they were young, and they had had a good meal about an hour before, but the body-crushing wind that sought out the many cracks in their armour, the whiplash effect of the sleet, and the apparent hopeless-ness of their quest made every step they took seem like a miracle. It was when Brian slipped and twisted his ankle that Margaret felt they would die. She remembers sitting down beside him, cradling him in her arms, not afraid any more. Nor did the cold seem so bad, and that told her that the end was close, but even that failed to awaken any emotion except a vague sense of regret that it should all end in so futile a way, after all their dreams. Brian was urging her to get up and to fetch help, or at least to save herself.

'If I go on, I'll drop in the next twenty yards, and we'll die separately,' she told him. 'Let's accept the inevitable – let's die together.'

Margaret says now, 'It sounds terribly romantic, doesn't it – the lovers pledging themselves again in the face of extinction, but it wasn't like that. I was just too weary and depressed, and I didn't want to be alone.'

Brian added, 'You can't imagine how desolate and hopeless it seemed and, worst of all, how preventable it had been. I felt I had killed Margaret out of conceit and incompetence, and that was a very bitter thing.'

As they lay together in the icy darkness, the light appeared again. Thinking it was an illusion, Margaret barely showed interest. Then a searchlight shot out from it, and they found themselves lit up. Brian, who was lying on his side, remembers feeling, rather than hearing, the vibration of a mighty engine. He likens it to the sound he used to hear as a boy when he put his ear to a railway line. The prospect of rescue poured new life back into them both, and they clambered to their feet. Blinded by the searchlight, they could not see what lay behind it. Margaret says she imagined it must be some moor rescue-patrol set up to look for idiots like them; Brian fancied it was an army unit that had stumbled on their car and come looking for them.

The searchlight went off abruptly, and they saw a tremendous building in front of them. It was four storeys high and over a hundred feet broad and seemed to be lit from the inside, like a giant curve of translucent polythene. A door opened, and three figures emerged, silhouetted in the light from inside. As they approached, they both had the curious feeling that there was something inhuman about them; on reflection, they agree that this could have been because the figures were very tall but slim to the point of emaciation. They were wearing surgical masks and black one-piece suits. They stopped a yard away, and then one stepped forward, handing a cup to each of them: 'Drink it. It will help.' They swallowed the liquid and were almost instantly filled with inner warmth and a tremendous sense of well-being. (Brian compares the drink to very fine brandy, but without any real taste, and not having any later side-effects.) As Brian stepped forward to return his cup, in an instinctive gesture of thanks, his ankle gave way again, and he fell heavily. The figure bent and ran his fingers along the leg. Then he rose. 'It is not serious.' He turned to Margaret. 'Can you drive?' She nodded, and the figure bent again and lifted Brian up – clearly being stronger than his frailty would suggest. It was a weird procession: the man with Brian in his arms, Margaret hurrying, almost running to keep up, and the two other silent figures following.

By now it had stopped snowing and the searchlight came on again to direct them to the car. The man placed Brian carefully into the passenger seat, then stood back to allow Margaret past to the driving-seat. 'Wait there. Do not move whatever happens; we are going to move you to a place of safety.' They thanked him profusely, but he just nodded, and the three walked back to the building. The door closed behind their benefactors, and they waited, expecting to see a truck appear from somewhere. What actually happened was that the 'building' began to rise from the ground; the lights dimmed and the great mass of the thing began to drift towards them with increasing speed. Brian says he was almost overcome with panic and wanted to jump from the car, but the man's words, 'Do not move – *whatever happens*', kept him where he was. It was on a collision course, and they both ducked as its vast bulk seemed to be about to come through the window. There was only a slight shiver from the car, and a sensation of movement all around, and they stared out of the windows to see if they had moved from the ditch. Utterly incredulously they looked down to see the moor dotted with tiny pinpricks of light and, here and there, larger concentrations. Coming up fast was a great sea of coloured lights, and they were swooping down towards it. Another barely perceptible jolt to the car, and they were in a quiet road in what turned out to be the outskirts of Plymouth. They sat there talking about the experience – they don't know for how long – then, still feeling warm and uplifted, continued their journey, with Margaret at the wheel.

Brian and Margaret both admit that they couldn't swear to what they actually thought about the people and the strange building before the fantastic rescue took place. They say that the events that followed have too much coloured their memories and that anything they said would probably be misleading.

That these creatures deliberately came to their aid is self-evident. Quite how they knew that the couple were in trouble in the first place is not so easily answered. Was the light that Margaret saw the UFO going about some covert operation in a place it considered safe? If that is so, its occupants showed remarkable decency in revealing themselves to people who would never otherwise have lived to tell the tale. And the stranger's mastery of English was flawless – which might be sinister, were it not for the gallant way in which he behaved.

There are a number of minor inconsistencies between their two stories (I have talked about the experience to them both together and separately). As with all my researches, couples who agree on every detail, and dot the Is and cross the Ts in the same place, don't get into the book. Knaves work their stories out too well; it is the honest who disagree. Without a doubt their story is true. I've talked to lots of people who have been in great danger, and to some who pretended to have been. There is a quiet intensity in the genuine ones as they talk about what happened, and I envy Brian and Margaret their encounter.

The Hangar in the Sky

Graham Rogers had been a navigator with a short-service commission in the RAF. During this time he had become determined to fly and had learnt as much as he could while in the Service. On his discharge, he had taken lessons and soon had a pilot's licence. He had a job as supervisor of a large chain of supermarkets, and this left him very little spare time. It was, however, a very well-paid job, and he soon managed to buy a secondhand light aircraft; it was his practice to fly her whenever he found a few hours free from work.

In June 1985 the opportunity came for him to take a whole afternoon off – a rare treat – and he intended to have a good look at his plane, make sure she was in fine form, then fly in the beautiful weather. As things turned out, he was later getting away than he had predicted, and it was getting on for evening by the time he was ready. Nevertheless, it was still wonderful flying weather and he had no hesitation in taking off. His flight plan was to take him well out over the North Sea, beyond his home county of Lincolnshire. The great fields of sugar beet and corn stretched below him, and he recalled his time as a boy when he and his friends would help with the pea-picking or collect strawberries and, best of all, help the farmers with burning the stubble in August.

The green suddenly gave way to blue as he took the plane out to sea. This was RAF country, and it was important to stick rigidly to one's programme. The Air Force did not take kindly to errant civilians, so he stuck firmly to his plan. The forecast was for storms later on but, as he flew on, the first ominous signs of a build-up of cloud were visible in front of him. It didn't look as if it were going to be too serious, but he began to climb to get above it. Without any warning he ran into very dense cloud, with lightning about. There was a flash that lit up his tiny cockpit, then he was clear of it. Rather relieved that it hadn't been worse, he decided to head for home, as the weather was clearly going to get worse ahead.

None of the instruments would respond; the engine still ran smoothly enough, but he had no control of anything. He felt afraid. There was enough fuel for another hour perhaps, yet it would only take him further and further out until, at last, the plane would nose-dive into the sea or the land. As far as he could calculate, the plane would take him over the northern tip of Norway and land him in the freezing waters beyond. He began to try to find the fault in the system, but without any success. The lightning had fused some cabling somewhere, and it was well beyond his reach.

The fear seemed to leave him, and he remembered many stories of other pilots who had been in seemingly doomed planes: as long as there was hope, the fear continued; once you came to terms with it, calmness returned. In the face of certain death, the mind adjusts and calms fears. It made biological sense, and Graham was a logical man. For all that, he was angry: if Fate had decided it wanted him dead, why hadn't it made a quick job of it, not left him an hour or more to think about it?

The minutes passed and he tried desperately to think of something useful to do with his time. He had paper and pen, but the chances of his being found at all were so remote that it seemed futile to write to his wife. His solicitor had his will, all his insurance was fully paid up, and there was nothing except sentiment that he could write down. As it happened, he didn't much care for his wife, and the feeling was mutual. He didn't really think much of his girlfriend either, and the thought made him smile rather grimly. He was going to his death without loving, or being loved by, anybody. It was rather a miserable way to go. To add to his wretchedness, there was no way of knowing when the engine would stop, as the indicators were not functioning.

The night was dark now, with just a glow on the horizon ahead. The storm had moved away, he could see the faint glimmer of a ship's lights below, and the stars were fantastic. A line from Dickens' *Barnaby Rudge*, when he thought he was going to die, came to him: 'We shall know what makes the stars shine, now.' Perhaps he would, although he had no formal belief in a life to come. The idea of praying did cross his mind, but he rejected it as unmanly. To refuse to acknowledge a Creator when things were going well, only to betray a lifetime's conviction when the going got tough, seemed despicable. Then the engine coughed, and it was like the last trump. A few more wheezes, and total silence filled his world; then there came the sound of the wind in the rigging, and the plane was going down.

To his right there suddenly appeared a bright light which he first took to be a lighthouse, before realizing that he was not down far enough to see such a thing. The light was closing with him fast, and he wondered if it was a NATO plane coming to investigate an interloper. That seemed unlikely, since he would have been on their screens for over an hour. Whatever it was was very close now, and for the first time he got some idea of the vastness of the thing. During his time in the RAF he had seen many strange things on radar, and it was an open secret in the Service that UFOs existed. He had himself listened in to them talking with other craft in a language it was impossible to understand. The British government, like those of nearly all the great powers, required personnel to report such incidents, but the official line was always that such sightings were misinterpretations of natural phenomena, a story guaranteed to rise a laugh in any Strike Command mess.

The bulk of the thing now blotted out all the stars to the right of his aircraft; then the light was above him. Below, the sea was rushing up with horrifying speed. The UFO was now travelling parallel to him, and a door opened in its side. The UFO shifted to the left, and he and his plane were suddenly inside the ship. He mentally took his hat off to the pilot of the strange vessel, who had manœuvred the giant thing to match exactly the speed and direction of the doomed plane and saved him from certain death.

Graham felt various changes in velocity, then lights came on in the compartment. It contained various machines, whose nature he could only guess at. He opened the cockpit, and a voice boomed out: 'Please leave your aircraft and go to the room indicated.' The indicator was a flashing light, and he climbed from the plane and made his way towards it. A door opened on his approach, and he entered a room furnished simply but comfortably. He sat on a chair, stunned. A few seconds earlier he had been facing extinction; now he was safe aboard an alien spaceship.

The voice came over again, from directly above him: 'Do you require medical treatment? If so, please state the problem. If you are well, do you require food or drink?'

He leant back in the chair. 'I'm OK physically, but I'd like a drink, please.' The voice had a touch of humour as it asked its next question: 'An alcoholic drink or water?'

He felt very relaxed with this voice. 'A whisky would be very nice, thanks.'

A few seconds later a door opened and a man entered with a large glass of whisky, which he placed on the table, then he sat down opposite. He was very tall and very thin (for comparison of description, see 'The Flying [Saucer] Doctors').

'We are mending your aircraft. The fault is minor. We shall refuel it and leave you close to the airfield you wish to return to.' The man's English was faultless, although spoken as all foreigners speak it, too purely.

'I've a million questions to ask,' Graham answered after he had taken a large swallow from the glass, to find it excellent Scotch.

The man smiled. 'I'm sorry. I have a set speech to make, but I won't answer questions. That is a rule of your own military, isn't it?'

Graham smiled back, quite at ease with this strange man. 'Yes, what's the speech, and why did you bother to save me?'

The man looked perplexed. 'We are not machines. If life

is threatened, we try to save it; that is what your race does. We were fortunate enough to be in your area and saw you were in trouble, so we helped.'

Graham said that he was grateful and asked for the speech.

The man smiled and said, 'We come from another star system, not from your Sun's planets. I can say nothing of our purposes, but we are not hostile. All planets go through more or less what is happening to you and, when that settles, we shall land and invite you to join our group. Tell whoever you like about our meeting; they won't believe you. Now I think your aircraft is ready. Would you please get back into it?'

Graham started to speak, but the man held up his hand, gesturing towards the door in friendly dismissal. Graham boarded his plane and at an appropriate moment the voice told him to switch on the engine. The UFO then tipped on its side and released his plane, and he was flying a few minutes from his home airfield.

Graham has no doubt that the UFO registered on NATO's screens as just another sighting to be recorded and forgotten. He will always remember the men who saved him and hopes that their official coming to the world will be in his lifetime, perhaps giving him a chance to thank those who saved him from the cruel sea.

Miscellany III:
A Collection of Curiosities

In the summer of 1967 a young man and his fiancée, Mark and Paula, were walking by the Thames near Henley. They were suddenly alerted by cries for help and ran towards the bank. Struggling in the water was a girl in a bright yellow dress, her hat still attached but floating behind her head. She was clearly in great difficulties, and the young man had no hesitation in diving in to rescue her. He could hear her cries getting louder and feel the movement in the water from her thrashing body, but when he got to where he thought she would be, there was nothing there. He turned to ask his fiancée where she had gone, thinking a current must have swept her off at a tangent, only to see Paula standing there in what appeared to be a trance. He shouted again and she snapped out of it. 'She's gone – she's not there any more,' screamed the frightened girl, and he returned to the shore. The river was completely unruffled.

'She just disappeared as you got close,' she gasped.

'You mean she drowned? Show me where. I may still get to her in time.'

He was angry with his fiancée for this seeming indolence in the face of an actual or imminent tragedy and, receiving no reply, dived in again and swam strongly towards the last place he had seen her. He dived repeatedly but finally confessed failure and returned to the shore. Paula had recovered much of her composure and insisted that the girl had not sunk – she had vanished. One moment she had been there, with water being splashed all around, the next instant there was perfect calm, and she had seen him alone in the water. Refusing to believe her, he alerted a man in a boat who was coming up river, to help him search for the girl. The man listened with apparent unconcern as they both shouted their stories.

He shook his head. 'I don't know where she is, but I'm sure it isn't at the bottom,' was his reply, and he told them that this was a comparatively regular occurrence, that a number of reports of the girl in yellow had been made over the years, sometimes resulting in elaborate searches. Nothing was ever found, nor had it ever been established who she had originally been.

There have been more than twelve sightings of this strange figure over the years, over quite a large stretch of the river. It is always in summer and during the afternoon. Whether she appears when no one is there is, of course, an impossible question to answer, and the significance of her appearance an equal mystery.

A Welsh clergyman has the strange ability to dream the winners of famous races – not only the outright winners but all first three horses. This first happened in 1963 and has continued intermittently ever since. He has been a lifelong opponent of gambling in every form, believing it to be a trick of the Devil.

He has been urged to use this good fortune, if not for himself, for some of the many good causes to which he has devoted his life. This he declines to do, arguing, quite logically from his own standpoint, that if it is the work of Satan, evil will come from it, no matter where the money goes. Stung by oblique taunts that his story is a fabrication, he has sworn another clergyman to secrecy and tells him about his dream before the race takes place. He is consistently right. He has seemed to be wrong sometimes, but a disqualification or a photo-finish has always vindicated his prediction.

There are analogies here to 'Surrey's Mother Shipton' and 'The Voice', but the selectivity of the information, horseracing only, its continuity over many years, and its constantly falling on stony ground leave us baffled to suggest any remotely probable explanation.

One of the most-seen ghosts in Britain is also, paradoxically, the least well-known, and I have to be extra careful in reporting this case for fear of suggesting the names of the entertainers alluded to.

Often when they appear on the stage, and sometimes on TV, there is one too many people in the troupe. This is never detected by the people on stage but has been noted by audiences and recorded on videotape. The figure is dressed as the others are dressed (it is a family show) and is that of a young girl. She dances and sings as part of the group, although always invisible to them. The father, maintaining the fiction that she *is* a member of the family, explains her occasional absences in various ways, and nobody questions it.

A child was born to them who lived only a few hours. Had she lived, she would be about the same age as the little girl. Whether it is she or some other ghost who has latched onto them for some inexplicable reason, we don't know. I have been allowed to see the family's birth records, and there is certainly one extra person on stage sometimes. The apparition never appears at any other time, and they cannot say, looking at the video, if there is any marked family resemblance. Curiously she is never at rehearsals, yet her performance is always polished. The father is at great pains to conceal this fact, as he already has enough trouble with managers and agents explaining this strange discrepancy. He has consented to have the story published only in the hope that someone has a credible explanation – which I will pass on.

We have already seen how a number of spirits find themselves quite at home with our modern devices, but in this next case the ghost is literally at home with a telephone and causes the owner of the house embarrassments similar to those of the theatrical father above.

Whenever he and his wife are out, the voice of an old lady answers the phone. She will only ever say that no one is at home, and will they please call back later. He and his wife have phoned her up countless times to try to persuade her to go away, but they get the same message. He has installed an Ansaphone, but to no avail, the little old lady still gets to the receiver before the machines takes over, even though it is set to make only two rings before the automatic equipment comes into play. His mother is dead, but the voice does not resemble hers in any way. The people who owned the house previously were two brothers, and there seems no connection with the house and the strange lady who monitors the phone. They place the voice as that of a woman of about seventy and have now become reconciled to her polite, but not very helpful, operator service.

On the subject of Reincarnation, a lot of research has been done by what is called hypnotic regression. Basically, this means putting patients under hypnosis and taking them back through their lives, a technique used to solve problems that developed in childhood. With regression in these cases, however, the process is continued back still further, into what are supposed to be other lives the person has led. There has been much nonsense published on the subject, but the idea does have its merits.

In the early 1970s an American researcher tried a major experiment. He enlisted the help of many people who were interested in the subject to assist in following up details of the alleged past lives that were revealed under this technique. What he was looking for was some fact passed on by an individual *which he could not possibly have known except by being alive at the time stated*. This, needless to say, proved a very tall order, and many seemingly fruitful lines of enquiry petered out without producing any significant evidence.

Eventually, however, he had a volunteer who appeared to be producing good material; as he went back, life by life, the amount of fact he was able to present became very formidable and convincing, but without that magic ingredient that would *prove* his previous incarnation. The method used was to have sessions at weekly or fortnightly intervals, pass the information gathered on to the field staff and then proceed with the next regression if things turned out satisfactorily. All subjects who remembered being Napoleon or Queen Victoria were politely eliminated at the start, but with this subject the previous incarnations followed a statistical pattern drawn up by the investigator. Simply put, he had worked out population ratio to job-opportunity and measured the subject's score against this. For instance, if a person were a shopkeeper or a whore more often than would be feasible on the law of averages, suspicion was aroused, because this would show a predilection for a specific role, suggesting an element of fantasy. (I can see the point, of course, although perhaps some souls were being groomed in a special way, but some sort of yardstick has to be adopted, and this seems a good one.)

When the researcher reached his subject's life in England at about the time when 'Bloody Mary' was succeeded on the throne by her sister Elizabeth I (1558), a most exciting event occurred. The subject, then called Drake (not Sir Francis), remembered being afraid of persecution of the Catholics by Elizabeth. Having no special preference, he had been a good Catholic under Mary and now wished to be a good Protestant under Queen Bess. Accordingly, he placed certain religious items in a sack and lowered them down a well on a string, which he secured out of sight from the top. They were small items such as crucifixes and images of the Virgin Mary that it would be unwise to have about if a witch-hunt against Catholics started. The expected persecutions did not arrive, so he decided to recover the items and sell them, since they were of some value. He found, however, that the string had rotted and the contents had plunged to the bottom of the well. The expense of recovering them from such a situation would have been more than they were worth, so he wrote it off to experience.

There now began the crucial task of finding where this well was, and this proved most difficult. He was closely questioned about the situation of his house, and the nature of his business – he said he was a corn merchant in Nottingham. By adroit use of local information, the site was gradually narrowed down to a small area, and the search began for a well, or record of a well. It did not look too hopeful, as a vast amount of development had gone on since the sixteenth century. By a stroke of luck, some old plans were discovered that showed the site of a well, but now built over, and further investigation was impossible. The plans had come to light only by chance and had most certainly not been disturbed in at least a century. An additional map revealed further evidence that the man's story was true: just by the site of the old well (not shown on this map) were marked some small buildings, and these were named as Drake's barns, suggesting the truth of his claim that he was a corn merchant.

When one considers that this subject's previous information had been very accurate and that he could not possibly have discovered the existence of the well or the additional map showing the barns that bore his name, I think that the reasonable man would consider the case for believing that some individuals lead a succession of lives thoroughly proved.

TIME TRAVEL

The Man who Gatecrashed a Roman 'Orgy'

In this century, almost every mystery that baffled our forefathers has had its wings clipped. We don't know everything, but there is nothing that we know nothing about, save the greatest enemy – time!

There are clocks that are only one second out in a million years, and we have learnt a lot of the operations of time. For instance, thanks to Einstein, we know that speed has an influence on time: if we were able to drive a spaceship at half the speed of light (by no means impossible within a few years), time for those on board would slow down relative to the outside universe; after a week in orbit around the Earth, the astronauts would return to find that much longer had elapsed for those they left behind; if speeds increased more, a day in space would finally represent millennia at home. This is not theory; by use of incredibly sensitive instruments, this has been proved on New York's Empire State building: because the top travels slightly faster than the base, clocks accurate to millionths of a second are found not to agree with one another when one is placed at the top, one at the bottom.

Nevertheless, although we are familiar with the effect, we have no inkling as to the cause. Time is still a mystery, and some scientists say that it doesn't exist in the same way as space or matter and that it is merely a human device to record change and the minutia of human affairs artificially. Whatever the reality, human history is littered with examples of those who can apparently see the future and, more rarely, catch glimpses of the past. Most of these have been either mistaken or corrupt, but enough evidence has come down to cause us to pause before rejecting everything as hokum. Names such as Nostradamus, Robert Nixon, Mother Shipton and St Malachi

have lasted, and in our own time the startling Jean Dixon*
has given much food for thought.

The events described in this report are of the rarest type
of experience, and very few similar instances are on
record. It is fortunate that the subject of the happening
was both an intelligent and a brave man. The point to be
considered above all is that this experience may be
relatively commonplace, but that the shock of it either
causes a breakdown of nerve in the subject or leads to
irrational action that results in death or serious injury,
thus preventing the person from making a safe return to
their own time. This subject's views on long-term
hauntings are horribly plausible.

Malcolm Turner is a statistician, running his own
successful company in Surrey. He is a PhD and an
ex-officer of one of Britain's toughest regiments – he had
good cause to bless this background one November night
in 1986.

It was a dreary night when Malcolm and his wife,
Evelyn, started out for a weekend with friends in Kent.
About three miles from home, Evelyn suddenly remembered that a box containing gifts for their host and hostess
was still in the stables. They turned back and were soon
home again. Malcolm pulled the car into the large yard, a
little way past the house, to the stables. They didn't keep
horses, and the buildings served a multitude of purposes.
It was Evelyn who noticed the lights.

'A good thing we came back, I seem to have left the
lights on.' Then she stopped. 'Did you ...?' Malcolm
nodded.

The meaning of this exchange was that the house was
equipped with a sprinkler system, but not yet the
outbuildings. Consequently, whenever they went away,
they switched off the power in these buildings to
minimize the danger of fire, of which Evelyn had a
particular horror. Malcolm well remembered throwing the

---

* Jean Dixon was a clairvoyant of great fame in the 1940s and 1950s,
having been virtually the personal soothsayer of US President F.D.
Roosevelt.

switch just before he closed the front door. So they had burglars.

Rather grimly he got out, carrying the stout club, like a baseball bat, he always kept in the car. He told Evelyn to turn the car round and, if it was intruders, to drive next door and phone the police. He went slowly towards the doors, convinced that the noise of the car would have caused them to make their escape already, but he was fully keyed up for a fight, should it come to that. As he got close to the doors, there was the sound of music and loud voices, and he came to the conclusion that perhaps hippies had taken over, having somehow found out about their weekend away. Grasping the club more firmly, he flung the door open and strode into the stables.

Evelyn remembers seeing this, and the great glare that shot out of the opening. The door, swung with such force, bounced back, and the scene was hidden from view. She prepared to drive next door, but at that moment the door opened again, and her husband appeared silhouetted against the bright background. Even as her hand moved to open the car door, the light began to fade, and by the time she got to him, the stable was dark again. Yet she could smell strange perfumes in the air, aromas she did not recognize, and from within the building she could just detect a sighing sort of sound, like that of voices heard far away, but then that too was gone, and she was alone with her husband again, being slowly soaked by the cold rain. Malcolm seemed to be in shock of some sort, and she hurried him towards the house, fearing that the intruders had injured him before making off. Safely inside, she made straight for the phone, to call police and doctor.

'Don't do that, dear.' The sound of his voice, seemingly all right, cheered her immensely, and she rushed into the room. He had a whisky in his hand, and he had poured one for her. 'Sit down, dear, and please be ready for something startling. You saw the light through the door, didn't you?' She nodded. 'And you saw the light inside when I opened the door, I suppose?' She nodded again. He sat down beside her, putting his arm around her proprietorially. 'Half an hour ago I thought I should never see you again.'

At this, Evelyn began again to think that he *had* been attacked, perhaps concussed, and was delirious, for half an hour earlier they had been driving back together. But something made her stay silent.

Malcolm was quiet too, for a few moments, then he said, 'I still can't believe it. If you hadn't seen the light too, I'd be convinced I was heading for the funny farm.'

Feeling afraid, she turned to him. 'What *was* in the stable?'

He shook his head. 'As far as I can make out, it was the officers' mess of a Roman army.'

She stared at him in horror. 'I'm going to get you to hospital, and get the police too,' she said, struggling to get up.

'Don't do that yet,' he said. 'Hear what I have to say. If you still think there's something wrong with my mind, I'll go to the hospital myself.' Then he settled back into the settee and told her his story.

'I opened the door, expecting to find a squadron of drug-crazed hippies, but at first there seemed to be no one there. There was plenty of light, but the place was very smoky, with bits of shimmering stuff dotted all over the place – like a heat-haze. I stood there trying to adjust my eyes, and the scene seemed to suddenly clear; it was just like something coming into correct focus under a microscope – one second a hopeless blur, next a perfectly sharp picture. The place was very big and seemed to be made of wood – it had a very temporary look to it – and steam was coming from an enclosed area at the far end.

The noise was terrific, and everybody – men and women – seemed very cheerful. They were in every stage of undress, from the stark naked to men fully armoured except for a helmet. They were drinking something from an assortment of pots and cups, and the whole place was lit by an immense fire and dozens of torches, most of which seemed to be giving off more smoke than light.

My first thought was that the place had been taken over by a group for a fancy-dress party, so I went over to the fellow nearest to me, a short, bearded chap, and shouted at him. He didn't acknowledge me, so I shook him by the shoulder. You can't imagine how I felt when my hand just

went through him. It made me look at the crowd with new
eyes. In the relatively poor light, I began to pick out things
that I had not noticed at first – things that couldn't
possibly have been assembled by any group in the short
time they had had while we were away. Great racks of
weapons, cauldrons of steaming food, garish regimental
colours painted on the wall. Then there were the clothes –
on those who bothered to wear any. Armour –
breastplates and greaves, plumed helmets, and there were
military standards and, above all, the place was much
bigger than our modest stables.

'Somehow or other, the fear seemed to disappear, to be
replaced by an intense excitement and interest. I knew
then, without any doubt, that this was real, and the
remote past, probably Roman. Slowly I set out on a
miniature voyage of discovery. I examined racked swords,
the vats of ale – or whatever it was, the jugs of wine, and
the great stewing-pots. Touch seemed to be the only sense
I was deprived of, because I could smell and see and hear
everything. The smell was overpoweringly of spices, and
threatened all the time to make me sick, although it never
actually got that bad. From time to time I tried again to
make myself known to these people, but always in vain.

'High up, at the far end of the hall, was a great raised
podium, draped in coloured cloth, a giant flag perhaps.
High above and shrouded in darkness I could see the
outline of the battle standard of the legion, if that is what it
was. I remember the feeling of awe that came over me as I
stood by the little incense-burner and looked up at a
genuine eagle of the Roman Empire, not just a sign of
military power but a holy object.

'Then I thought of you, and of our home, and I started to
shiver, because I thought I might be trapped there, and I
thought of all those stories of places haunted for centuries
by the same restless, unhappy spirit. Perhaps, I imagined,
they were people like me, who had wandered into some
time-warp, only to be trapped there for ever.

'Feeling rather horrible, I made my way back to the
opposite end of the room, where I had come in. It was
very dark and gloomy, and the wall looked like a sheet of
steel instead of flimsy wood. In front of where I stood, a

small group of soldiers were playing dice, and I stood watching them. After one throw, which must have been particularly bad, one of the men let out what was obviously a Roman oath and flung the dice-box towards me. Laughing, the officer who had apparently won got up and strode after it, his eyes casting around in the semi-dark for it. He was almost level with me when he looked up, his face only a foot away from mine. He was clean-shaven, with a broad, squarish sort of face, and thick blond hair – a German, I should guess. He looked astonished, then frightened, and turned away, bellowing. At that, the others came blundering forward, and I instinctively stepped away, caught my heel on something and fell backwards against the wall, and I was back in this world again. Then you came down and brought me in. That's all really. What do you think?'

Evelyn believed the story. She had seen the light and smelt the spice, even heard what was the dying sound of the party as it slid back to wherever it had come from. She cancelled their weekend visit, and in the morning they examined the stable minutely. There was nothing to be seen, as Malcolm knew there would not be. Whatever evidence there might be of his visit to a Roman dining-in night, it was in a far-off time or buried forever under the ground on which they stood – or both.

A week later they heard what seemed to be shouting coming from the stable, but Malcolm did not go to investigate again, fearing that this time he might not get back. From then until the time of writing (March 1989) no further visitations have occurred, to their knowledge.

What is peculiar is that not only did Malcolm witness the events of another age but he seems to have had a time-scale different from Evelyn's. She says he was in there only a second or two; he is sure he was in there for over an hour. Indeed, to have seen all he did see, in such detail, he *must* have been there for more than a few seconds, and it seems likely that this other world was running at hundreds of times normal speed, so that the figures were effectively invisible until he had adjusted to their wavelength, as it were. Yet he was there sufficiently in body to smell things, fall over things and be seen as some sort of apparition by the soldier. Likewise, the light, smell and sounds were all relayed to Evelyn, albeit in a watered-down form. They agree that the shouting a week later (exactly a week) was probably imagination, but who can say?

Like so many such experiences, it is exciting, but that is about all. It tells us nothing and certainly raises more questions than it answers. More dishearteningly, it has not acted as any sort of revelation or inspiration for either Malcolm or Evelyn. For all that, it remains probably the best-documented and most solid event of its kind and should compel us to revise our hard-and-fast prejudices on the whole subject of time.

The Armada Ship

John Jefferies, under his pen name, is a successful author. His experience does have something in common with the incident in Surrey with the Roman legionary mess, but it introduces some novel aspects of the phenomenon.

John spent two years, 1977–9, writing his first book, working on it during the evening and at weekends. When it was a success, his wife, Stella (who had been a tower of strength during its creation), suggested that he resign from his job and that they rent a house for six months in a secluded place, where he could work on his new ideas. He had a very good position with a large company and was set to become a senior member of staff before much longer, probably ending up on the board of directors, so he was reluctant to throw aside such a secure and financially rewarding future on the strength of just one success, but finally Stella persuaded him. His employers were most reluctant to see him go and agreed to a six-month unpaid leave of absence, after which time John would be able to make a final decision. He was much relieved that he was not compromising Stella's future by pursuing his own career as a writer.

They let their London flat for a substantial rent, took a huge cottage in the west of Scotland for about a quarter of the price, and went off to their temporary home in excellent spirits. They had seen photographs of the house, and friends who lived in Edinburgh had looked it over carefully so that when they arrived, after a prodigious drive, everything was in order and ready for them to start work the next morning: John on his novel, Stella on a series of articles about the wildlife and plants in the area. A lady from the nearby village came in to make the bed, tidy the house, cook lunch and prepare the evening meal. But no amount of persuasion could get her to come in during the evening and when, after a week, they sent out invitations for a dinner party to a number of people they had got to know in the village, they were astonished to find that everyone had some excuse for not coming. It was left to a chance conversation overheard by Stella in a nearby town to explain this seemingly unsociable behaviour.

'The bay has a reputation for ghosties and ghoulies and especially for things that go bang in the night,' Stella explained on her return. 'The woman who was speaking would have said more, but I think she tumbled who I was.' Stella has a degree in anthropology and was a committed rationalist; John was less certain and more open to persuasion.

The months rolled by and John finished one book and made extensive drafts of two more, while Stella poured out a series of articles for a press that seemed unable to get enough of her work. The first book was enthusiastically snapped up for a considerable sum, and much interest was shown in the ideas for the other two. Discussions of film rights began almost immediately and, to crown Stella's faith, she was asked to be the guiding spirit of a major TV wildlife series. Fortune had certainly shone on them both, and the venture had paid off remarkably well. It was now the middle of August 1979, and the lease on the cottage terminated in the middle of September, so they decided to spend the last three weeks enjoying themselves while the good weather held. They visited local beauty spots and places of geographical and historical interest, attended theatrical performances put on by amateur reps, dined out a lot and generally relaxed after a punishing schedule of work.

On 2 September there was heavy rain all day. John ran their daily help home just after three and settled down to do the crossword in the sitting-room. Stella was correcting some proofs that had arrived that morning, and the only sound was the drumming of the rain on the windows of the house. This was suddenly broken by what sounded like a very loud pistol-shot, rapidly followed by another. Thinking it might be a maroon, John pulled on a coat and went outside. Immediately in front of him, in the cove, was a huge sailing-ship. Its sails were still fully extended, and it was these that were making the noise as they flapped in the wind. The rigging was thick with men attempting to reef them, and at the other end of the vessel some sailors were lowering a boat into the water.

John says that he felt only interest in what he thought was a tall ship exercising its crew. It was, he says, a few minutes before he noticed that the rain had stopped and that the sun was shining brilliantly. His attention had been totally absorbed by the novel sight of the ship, but now that he took his eyes off it for a moment to call Stella, a very curious situation met his eye. On the other side of him, just a few hundred yards away, the rain was still beating down fiercely, and the clouds were black and ominous. The sun was shining over an area only about a thousand yards in diameter, of which the ship was at the centre. The gig had put to sea and was being rowed rapidly toward the shore.

John called for Stella, and she came out, as open-mouthed as he. It was she who noticed that the wind that was blowing on them and the ship was in the opposite direction to the movement of the clouds and the trees across the cove, outside the area of the circle. She hurried back indoors for binoculars and camera, while he waited with growing apprehension for the arrival of the boat. One part of his mind was certain that they would be ordinary sailors, while the other part was in dread of them. The local fears about the cove, the inexplicable sunlight and the contrary winds, all served to arouse his primitive fears of the unknown. Stella returned with the binoculars but no camera. She had used the last of the film the night before and had been intending to buy replacements when they went into town the next day. Being on holiday had blunted her instincts for her job, as she would never normally be without plentiful supplies of spare film. She looked at the ship and passed John the glasses.

'It's a Spanish battleship,' she whispered, as though saying it out loud might make something awful happen.

'Shall we make a run for it?' he asked, but she shook her head.

'The best camouflage is to keep still. They probably haven't seen us, and we'd only draw attention to ourselves.'

Both recalled later the total lack of any unreality about either the scene or their own feelings. They seemed, they said, to have accepted that a ship from a period nearly 400 years before was anchored in their cove and that sailors were coming ashore who had no love for England. I asked them what made them think it was a hostile ship. Stella said that her look through the glasses had revealed extensive damage and hasty repairs to much of the superstructure and that it seemed the most natural thing in the world to assume that it was a ship escaping from the trouncing it had received off Calais at the hands of Queen Elizabeth I's navy.

The longboat beached itself less than fifty yards away, and the sailors began to unload empty water-casks. They looked tired and dispirited, many of them obviously suffering from wounds. The officer in charge looked barely out of his teens, terribly anxious, his eyes darting from left to right, his hand clutching a formidable-looking pistol. Then he caught sight of John and Stella, and they feared he would fire. Neither had any doubt that the bullet would be as real as the sounds and sights they were witnessing. He shouted something and pointed to the barrels. John had the presence of mind to point to a well in the garden. At this the officer put away the gun, and the whole party rushed the barrels up the gentle slope towards the unmistakable outline of the well. The couple watched them drink their fill from the bucket, the officer last, before they set to filling up with water for the rest of the ship. They worked at break-neck speed, the young officer like a cat on hot bricks. One by one the barrels were rolled down to the longboat and stowed, until the watering was complete.

John says that that was the crucial time as far as he was concerned: the Spanish officer would be perfectly justified by his own lights in killing them both in order to prevent them raising the alarm. In fact, quite the reverse happened – the young man doffed his hat in salutation before scrambling into the boat as it was pushed away from the shore. They watched the barrels being winched aboard, two being broached right away for a motley collection of wounded sailors who made their way aft either on makeshift crutches or swathed in bandages. The sails were set and the giant ship began slowly to make her way out to sea. With no warning whatsoever, she disappeared, and John and Stella found themselves standing in a drenching downpour.

John recalls how he put his arm around Stella as they watched the rain wash away the prints of the sailor's bare feet and the deeper indentations of the officer's boots. Then the ridges made by the filled barrels disappeared under the watery onslaught, and finally the great gouge made by the longboat was washed away from sight.

This story has to force us completely to rethink our conceptions of time. As with the case of the Roman mess, but much more so, we have one era impinging on another to the extent that they co-exist as realities in their own right, and both sets of people can see and communicate with each other. It had been an obvious but unprovable fact, believed by philosophers for many years, that the viewing of time as a series of events that ceased to be the instant they had happened was not a likely one. It is a sad fact that, of all the phenomena we encounter in the universe, the one that has the most effect on us is the one we know the least about. Even that remark is misleading, because we know nothing about time, except how to measure it, and that is not an exact science, as the 'velocity' of time, as it were, is dependent on the velocity of the object being timed. As things stand in modern science, time is effectively seen as a by-product of space or, more properly, the changes that take place in the physical world. This report is only one of hundreds of incidents from man's history that show how severely wrong we are in our ideas of what time actually is.

The Armada was finished off as a fighting force around 8 August 1588. Many of the ships limped away up the North Sea, then south, between Ireland and Scotland, to reach Spain by a roundabout route, well out of the reach of Admiral Lord Howard of Effingham and the likes of Drake and Hawkins. In this case, the ship seems to have appeared at about the time of year it would originally have arrived, but this may be a coincidence. My investigations among local people suggest that strange events linked with that stretch of water are by no means confined to late summer or daytime.

The Girl in the Wall

This is a most remarkable incident, for a number of reasons. The spirit was selective in who it appeared to, and it was of great antiquity, yet seemed to respond to what a modern human being said to it. I have spoken to all four of the players in this sad and terrible case, and there can be no doubt that the story I am about to relate is a completely genuine example of a haunting of the first magnitude.

Sarah Hunt had inherited a large house, not far from Leeds. It had been in the family for over 200 years and had once been surrounded by many hundreds of acres; most of these had been sold off to local farmers, but it still stood completely isolated in about five acres, given over mostly to trees and a small artificial lake. When Sarah married, she and her husband Brian decided to make it their permanent home and gradually to change it, so that it was a more suitable habitation for the family they intended to have. When she discovered she was going to have a baby, they decided that it was time to start renovations of the house.

To the right of the building, there was what was euphemistically called 'the barn', which comprised a group of shoddy outbuildings erected on the skeleton of some decayed stonework; at one time it may have been part of the house, but no one could remember. Sarah had grown up in the house, and the tumbledown structure had been old when she was a child. There were, however, substantial foundations, and it was their idea to clear the site and have a large nursery and playroom built, and a spacious flat for a live-in nanny. On the first floor they planned a suite of rooms in which to live while the insides of the old house were removed and it was turned into a modern dwelling.

It was late spring 1976 when the work began, and this gave Sarah reason to go into that part of the house long abandoned as too damp. Here was the door that connected the house with the 'barn' – a door which had long been sealed up to prevent rats finding their way in. On the first occasion she was there, measuring, she thought she heard a girl crying; the sound seeming to come from behind the door but, on inspecting it from the outhouse side, she found nothing. At another time she heard a low, fierce chant – 'like a prayer', she said, yet uttered in a horribly manic fashion. It seemed to be in a foreign language, yet with a curious interspersing of English. She found it unnerving and decided to get the contractors to do the job. She didn't tell anyone, although she did enter it in her diary, along with all the other events of each day – a habit she had had from childhood. (This was to be invaluable, as it allowed me to compare two independently experienced sides of the same haunting.)

The site was cleared, and the framework of the new house was raised. The morning after the workmen began putting up the brick walls, the foreman came with a curious complaint. During the night someone had kicked down all the fresh brickwork. As they lived down a lane, about half a mile from the nearest small village, this seemed an odd act of vandalism. The bricklaying was begun again, and the next morning it had once again been knocked down, with the added insult of a bag of cement's having been tipped over the fallen bricks. The police were called and admitted bafflement but promised to increase their patrols for the next few nights. All this was of no avail: the walls were flat again the next morning. Telling the contractor to build them up yet again, Brian announced his intention of spending the night concealed in the shrubbery. Sarah wouldn't hear of his staying there alone – if there were prowlers about, she wanted to be with her husband; he was equally adamant that she shouldn't keep watch with him. The impasse was resolved by Brian's calling in Donald, an old friend from their days together at Oxford, who was a rugby player and an amateur boxer and what used to be called 'a tough egg'. He jumped at the chance, and they arranged for him to come for dinner. To their surprise, he brought his wife, Annette, who had been a WRAF PTI officer and who knew quite a bit of judo. They were, indeed, a formidable pair, and during dinner Brian and Sarah were much amused by imagining the consternation of the hooligans when those two materialized out of the darkness. It is significant, but wasn't known at the time, that Annette was also pregnant.

All four went out about nine o'clock, while it was still quite light, to see the lie of the land. Over the annexe that was to be the nanny's flat, the workmen had thrown a few sheets of tarpaulin to make a shaded area where they could have their lunch and tea breaks. (1976 was the year of the very hot summer, when the government appointed a Minister for Drought.) They blew up their air-bed, Sarah brought out a couple of blankets, some sandwiches and a flask of coffee, and the pair settled for their vigil, although it would be a short night, getting light just after four. Despite his wife's advice, Donald had insisted on having a second large glass of port after dinner and, as a consequence, was rather sleepy. Annette, on the other hand, was wide awake, so she took the first watch. She decided to wake him at first light, then go into the house and sleep in a proper bed.

The night was very warm and very still. Annette knew she would get ample warning of anyone's approach, so she thought she would walk about a bit to stop getting stiff. She went barefoot, so as to give no indication of her presence and, as it was a dark night, she didn't feel that she would be jeopardizing her plan. When she went past the wall, she suddenly felt terribly cold, and her surroundings changed completely. She was in a room, with moonlight pouring through a grille in the roof, although there had been no moon when she entered. The end of the room, where the side of the house should be, was not visible. She turned, but behind her was another wall of equally massive stones, glittering with frost. She remembered her training and breathed deeply and slowly to fight down the panic – she admits that she had never been so scared.

A door opened in the far left-hand corner, and four figures entered, one carrying a huge torch of flames and applying it to three more attached to the walls, so that the chamber became quite brilliantly lit.

The newly entered figures were not the only people in the room. Sitting on a rough bed was a girl, aged about fifteen, Annette estimates, very pretty, with blonde hair, cut very very short and standing up in disarray. She was wearing only some tattered rags, her face was tear-stained and afraid; her hands were tied behind her. Annette found her instinctive sympathy with the girl overcoming her own fears and watched with mounting horror as two women, only the ovals of their faces showing in the blackness of their clothes, dragged the girl to her feet. It was immediately obvious that the girl was eight or nine months pregnant and that she was shouting something. Three of the figures were these black-coated women, the fourth a stunted old man carrying a bucket of some kind. Annette could see the girl's mouth moving in what were obviously screams and protestations. She was dragged across to an alcove, where a number of chains were set into the wall, and the two women began to secure her body and feet to the wall. The third woman passed the torch to the old man and pulled a heavy book from under his arm. She opened it and, running her finger slowly along the lines, began to read out something. Annette, however, had eyes only for the young girl, who was hanging forward in the chains, her body racked with sobs. The fact that people were obviously talking and shouting, yet emitting no sound, gave an added depth to the ghastliness of the scene.

The woman finished reading from the book, took back

the torch and pointed to the old man. He scurried forward, and Annette saw that a large pile of stones was heaped up against the wall. With hideous dexterity, the old man began to wall up the alcove, deftly piling brick upon brick, and applying mortar from the bucket with great speed and skill. In less than a minute, the girl was hidden from view. Only a tiny aperture was left, and the man reached up to place the last stone, but the woman laid a restraining hand on his arm. Then a snuffer was produced, and darkness closed in again over that dreadful wall entombing the girl. Slowly the procession made its way out by the door through which it had come, and only the moonlight remained.

Their departure seemed to release Annette from a spell, and she leapt forward to tear down the bricks, but her fingers touched only the outer wall of her friend's house and, once again, there were stars and trees and the warmth of the June night. Sobbing with revulsion as much as fear, she rushed back to awaken Donald. He was convinced that she had been dreaming, but the sight of the now demolished wall made him wonder, although Annette herself had not been conscious of hearing or seeing the collapse. They sat together for the rest of the night, but nothing more happened. As soon as they decently could, they went back into the house and, over breakfast, Annette related her story. It was then Sarah's turn to tell her experiences, and the company broke up in sombre mood.

As it was Saturday, Brian called the local vicar to ask for a ceremony of exorcism to be conducted, but the first opportunity would not be until Monday. All four had pledged themselves to secrecy; none of them wanted the notoriety or the considerable risk of spending the rest of their lives in the town with the term 'crank' attached to them, Brian and Sarah having the added incentive of not wishing to drive away the builders.

During the rest of the weekend, Sarah became more and more troubled; she had seen exorcisms on TV documentaries and in films, and it seemed to be a very abrasive and hurtful thing to do to the spirit of this wretched young girl, who had already been treated in the most abominable way. As a result of her thoughts, she embarked on a scheme which I think is the bravest thing I have ever encountered, and which I don't think I could have done myself, for any consideration. On the Sunday night she stayed awake and about 12.30 put on her dressing-gown and slippers and went quietly out to the shell of the new house. She stood facing the wall where the girl had been bricked up, and spoke to her. She doesn't remember exactly what she said, but the gist of it was this:

'I know your story, and I'm sorrier than I can say. But these walls are for life, not death. They are a new house for *my* baby. Nothing can bring yours back to you, or make up for the terrible things those people did. But that was very long ago. Things are different now. We don't let people do that sort of thing any more. If you want to stay here, I will be your friend and talk to you and try to help you, but isn't all life, in a body or out of it, something that moves on and moves up? Whatever is the next step in your journey, it can't be worse than this brooding on wrongs done centuries ago. Take my hand and see if my strength can help you make the break from this dreadful existence.'

She says that she felt the girl's presence, hesitant but not aggressive, and walked slowly forward, with her arms fully extended. Then she felt, for a few seconds, her hands gripped tightly, and the touch was warm and soft, with all malice and anger gone from it. Then the grip lessened, and the hands seemed to slide off hers as though the person were drifting away and the spirit was gone for ever.

When I did a little research, I discovered that there had been a religious house of some kind on the site at Henry VIII's dissolution of the monasteries, and there is evidence that it was used as a barn or cowshed for a long time, until the original Mr Hunt bought it in the middle of the eighteenth century.

The medieval practice of walling up nuns or novices who became pregnant was not common, but it happened. There is one revealing incident in Annette's account that leaves me in no doubt as to the truth of her story: it is where she tells of the woman's stopping the man from placing the last stone. I don't think the fact is known outside the most elite historical circles, but it was the custom of some orders of nuns to leave their victim to die lingeringly of hunger and thirst, rather than relatively quickly of asphyxiation, the pretext for this sadistic behaviour being to allow the sinner more time for repentance. It is a dreadful thing, but what the nun was reading to the girl was probably the burial service, a refinement of cruelty hard to believe.

The Disappearance of Peter

The events that were to overtake Peter Williamson on the evening of 28 July 1974 have many equals in history. What actually happened and precisely where he went for the three days that are unaccounted for must remain speculative, but there are some theories.

Foremost among these is the parallel universe concept. This was first mooted by German mathematicians in the nineteenth century and, broadly, the idea is that this universe of ours has many, perhaps an infinity of, similar universes that co-exist in the same space and time. An analogy for this can be found in a radio set: the world is full of radio waves, all jumbled together, yet we can isolate a particular wave by using the tuner. The idea that whole universes behave in the same way is a strange and awesome one, but it is not against any scientific principle. As with our radio, some problem in the ionosphere can cause another station to interrupt the one we are listening to, and by the same token it is suggested that interference with the delicate fabric that separates these universes can result in their allowing movement between themselves. This is probably a rare thing, but, as with other phenomena dealt with in this book, not as rare as the scientific establishment would like us to believe. There are, for instance, two well-documented cases, one in Spain and the other in Britain, in which green children have appeared, speaking the local dialect but unable to eat normal food. Interestingly, both sets of children reported that they had entered caves in their own land, only to emerge in ours. This is thought significant, because it is inside a mountain that we find the greatest stresses; the gravitational effects and a possible increase in the magnetic field would be inclined to warp a wall of energy more than conditions in the open, as in this case, lightning was the catalyst.

It is unfortunate that so many people disappear for perfectly rational reasons, because it gives us no opportunity to isolate those cases where something odd has been at work. If we were able to return to a period where human civilization was hyperstatic (the Dark Ages, for example), we should no doubt find that there were a large number of disappearances without the convenient explanations we have today. At least one report exists that tells of regular masses being said in most villages for souls stolen by the Devil during the year. In our own time, if you bother to read the small stories in newspapers, some very peculiar things emerge. People who have lost their memories or who are mentally deranged are always turning up and, in a significant number of cases, no success is forthcoming from efforts to find out who they are. I am not given to seeing mysteries everywhere, or to subscribing to conspiracy theories, but human nature itself is the best preventer of any curiosity, let alone scientific investigation, being generated by these events.

Nobody expects to be murdered, and nobody expects to come across people from flying saucers, the next world or parallel universes. We all say that we keep an open mind, but this isn't really true. Because we all have the 'It can't happen to me' attitude and don't want to run the risk of making public idiots of ourselves, we let things pass by without comment. It is only when our noses are rubbed in something and there is no real way of closing our eyes that we sit up and take notice.

This was certainly the attitude of Peter's friends, who, by their own admission, were pressured only by their proximity to the strange events into accepting that something outside normality had taken place.

On the evening in question, Peter had arranged for some friends to come round for drinks and a barbecued meal. Being quite wealthy, he lived in a large house in

Somerset, with his wife and two children, and all four were present at the beginning of the party. (It is in this that his case bears a superficial resemblance to that of David Lang in America a hundred years before. Lang also disappeared in front of his wife and two children but he never returned.)

As the guests were warming up with their drinks, there was a sudden storm, but the patio area was well covered, so the party continued without interruption. Blue sky was visible beyond the clouds, and the storm's arrival was generally considered welcome, the evening being very humid and oppressive. At the height of the rain, one of the children noticed their pet, a dog called Scruff, cowering under a bush. Peter told the child to stay put and darted out to rescue the terrified creature. Half way across the lawn, he was suddenly silhouetted by a terrific flash of lightning that forked down to destroy a tree in a neighbouring garden. Almost every eye was turned towards him when, with no sound, he simply vanished from sight. Mary, his wife, screamed, the children burst into tears and the guests poured onto the lawn in search of him. Despite their combing every inch of the garden, there was nothing of any kind to be seen, and the police were called. They made their own intensive search of the house and garden, but equally found nothing. Mary was put under sedation, and the children stayed with friends. Two of the men remained behind, taking alternate watches through the night, in case Peter should return.

No one had any idea of what had actually happened, and the police explanation was becoming more acceptable by the hour, despite experience to the contrary. In a nutshell, this 'explanation' was that the lightning strike had occasioned a trauma of some sort, causing amnesia or disorientation. The illusion of a sudden disappearance was caused by the watchers' being temporary blinded by the flash and imagining that no interval had elapsed between the lightning and the disappearance, whereas in reality a minute or two had passed, during which time Peter had walked away. All this came to be believed by most of the guests, despite the fact that the whole garden was surrounded by a very high wall and that the only way in or out, a door by the garage, had been locked by Mary because the latch was broken and it banged in the slightest breeze. The key was found in her pocket, and there were no marks anywhere on the wet earth that ran the entire circuit of the wall to suggest that anyone had attempted to climb it, which would have been a lengthy and difficult job, even under ideal circumstances, there being no trees, just flimsy trellis with such delicate plants as fuchsias, on which no marks or damage could be found.

It is in the nature of such cases that those involved latch on to any explanation, rather than confront the mystery head on, and almost without exception this ludicrous solution to the problem became current. It had the advantage, of course, of leaving Peter alive and well somewhere and did not threaten anyone with the disquieting thought that it could happen to them or their loved-ones.

A search and alert were put out around the neighbourhood, and later extended nationwide, with TV pictures and news stories. All this elicited nothing, and people settled down to a long wait, perhaps recalling the amnesiac Ronald Colman in *Random Harvest*, who disappears and takes up a new life for years.

On the third day, the gardener discovered Peter lying in some shrubbery, one foot immersed in a small ornamental pool. Although it was only eight in the morning and that part of the garden was quite secluded, Peter's clothes were dry (the gardener was emphatic on the point), with no sign of dewfall on them, suggesting that he had certainly not been there during the night. Once again, the circumstances are curious, as an inventory of the possessions on him shows no sign of a key (the gardener had his own), yet he had apparently managed to get into the garden (according to the police) via the road, although, once again, no marks of an entry were visible. On his being taken to hospital, it was found that he was suffering from loss of memory, and because the authorities had been right in one particular, it was irrationally assumed that they must be right in all, and the matter was settled in people's minds.

After a week Peter was discharged from hospital, fit and

well but still unable to recall where he had been for the mysterious three days. There the matter might have rested, if it had not been for the dreams; these began shortly after his return home and, as he described them, related to a time he seemed to have spent in another place, very like his home area.

Before dealing with the remarkable revelations that were to come, I should like to pause to go a little further into the theory of parallel universes, to acquaint readers with the supposed nature of such places, the better to illuminate Peter's experiences. The idea is that all these alternative creations began from a common root and evolved along the same lines, changing only when some interval event that is unique to that universe takes place. For instance, all nature would behave uniformly in all universes; the only events that might be different are those where there is an exactly 50–50 chance of something going either way. In that instance, a tree might fall to the right in one system and to the left in another; if a young man were standing to the right, he would be killed in only one universe, and as a result his family would not be born. This would multiply in complexity, resulting in a radically different situation. In large examples – if the man were Columbus, for instance, – the whole structure of the planet's politics and economy would be different, leading to a world utterly alien to the one we know. However, examples where there was an *exactly* even chance of two or more possibilities occurring are very rare indeed, and the consensus of opinion between scientists interested in the theory is that there would be little difference between those universes that are adjacent to our own, and that only in remote systems, where unusual events have had the opportunity to multiply, would significant changes be visible.

In his dreams, which were of the lucid variety, Peter found himself soaking wet, in the middle of a garden, with no memory of anything that had gone before. He could recall coming to, standing among some flower beds, near a small road. Feeling frightened, he had wandered down the road, half anxious to tell someone his troubles, yet half afraid. He had walked for a long time in the evening light until he felt faint and sat down by the side of the road. Here a passing doctor had stopped to offer help, and he had driven Peter to hospital on discovering the nature of the problem. Dressed only in a pair of jeans and a T-shirt and carrying nothing by which he could be identified, he had been put to bed and the police sent for. He could tell them nothing, and they went away saying that they would check their Missing Persons files. The doctor who was attending him was called Nugent, and the sister was Alice Charles; he also remembered the names of various nurses, and the name of the ward, Pritchard.

The dreams were uneventful and quite unlike the normal nocturnal fantasies in which the brain plays fast and loose with logic and reality. He simply had memories of a stay in hospital, but of such normality that he felt he must be remembering actual events that had occurred while he had lost his memory. One curious and dreamlike memory of his stay in the hospital was that he seemed to be having hallucinations. From time to time the ordinary scenes of the ward would seem to shimmer, and a set of faces and furniture would appear, entirely different from those that were normally there. These glimpses were only momentary, but he had spoken to the doctor about them and had been examined for any signs of concussion, it being thought that a blow or a fall was the most likely cause of the amnesia. Nothing was found, however.

One other thing that Peter recalled was that, although he seemed to be speaking normally, the words appeared to be almost a drawl compared with the crisp speech of the doctor and nurses. In his own words, it was just short of 'slow motion'. In the afternoon of the second day he was allowed to get up for a short walk in the grounds. There was a slight problem when the sister reported that his jeans were too battered and muddy to be wearable and had been burnt. A Cornishman in the next bed came to the rescue and lent him a pair of corduroy slacks for as long as he should need them. In the dreams he had a walk, went to the hospital café for some tea, read a book and went to sleep. The police had been back that evening to see if he remembered anything and to report on their progress. This had been presented in a most hopeful light but actually amounted to a total blank.

The following morning he felt altogether better, although he still had no inkling of who he was. Feeling restless, he decided to take a stroll in the gardens before breakfast. Finding them soggy from overnight heavy rain, he struck out over the open country along a nearby road. Very quickly the scene became familiar, and he realized that he was close to the point where he had first been aware of having no memory. Curiosity overcame him and he decided to have another look, on the off-chance that there would be something there to tell him who he was. The last memory of the dream was of walking over some turf towards the garden from which he had emerged.

This remembered sequence of events was built up piecemeal over a period of about three weeks, with nothing some nights, a lot the next, and many repetitions. The images were so vivid that Peter began to wonder if he had not, in fact, been in such a place during the three days. Of course, knowing nothing of his disappearance, he had not contradicted the explanation that was now the accepted wisdom. Busy with his work, he had relatively little time to dwell on the matter or to make any enquiries until, one Sunday in August, his son asked to be taken to a motorcycle rally being held nearby. Remembering a previous visit and the appalling muddiness of the place, Peter went to put on some old clothes. He was searching for his jeans when the penny dropped: he should no longer have had them – they had been burnt in his dream. If the dream was not a dream, he should have a pair of corduroy trousers that belonged to someone else.

Peter quickly found them, cleaned and pressed in his wardrobe. His wife had brought him a suit when he left hospital and must automatically have had these trousers cleaned, their significance being lost in the excitement of his homecoming. They were obviously expensive, and he felt a pang of guilt that they had not been returned. Not only that, but if he could trace the owner, he could find out which hospital he had been at, thank all concerned for their help and explain that he was now OK. There was a label inside, indicating a Herbert Fox of a well-known West Country town, with a set of monogrammed initials,

JB, sewn into the label – initials such as the older generation used to have sewn on the maker's label, much like an up-market laundry mark. Quite elated, he tried to get the tailor's name from Directory Enquiries, but it was unlisted. Anxious, now that the trail was hot, he decided to drive down to the town and get the information in person. It was a hundred-mile trip, but it would be worth it to discover the truth of those lost days. There is, he confided in me, nothing more upsetting than having a time in your life utterly unaccounted for.

It was a smallish town and enquiries soon established that no such shop existed. In desperation, he tried the local Chamber of Trade. The shop had existed but had been burnt down in the 1950s and had never reopened. Totally bewildered, he returned home. The trousers were new, and they were in the current styling – they could not have come from the fifties, no matter how carefully they had been kept. He was now so wound up about the whole matter that he enquired whether there were any towns in the Commonwealth or the US that had that name, but without success.

It was there that the mystery might have stayed, except for a chance meeting with a friend who lived a couple of miles away. He had recently been in hospital for a minor operation, and when the name Nugent cropped up, it was eagerly followed up by Peter. Where was this hospital? It was the cottage hospital in his own town, was the reply, not half a mile from where he lived. He had not known of this place, having been taken to the larger general hospital on the insistence of one of his guests, a prominent local doctor.

Peter lost no time in visiting the small hospital, tucked away on the outskirts of the town. He was sure it was the place long before he reached it – all the landmarks close by seemed familiar, and he remembered the road he had taken on his final walk from the place. Inside, his dream became reality and it was exactly as he remembered it. He asked at reception for Dr Nugent and was asked to wait. A few minutes later the friendly face of the man who had spent so much of his time trying to help came into view.

'You wanted to see me?' There was no flicker of

recognition whatsoever. Peter explained his purpose, but the doctor shook his head. 'I'm afraid you have the wrong hospital. I've never seen you before, and I haven't had an amnesia case for five years.'

He took Peter to the tiny tea-room, they sat down and the doctor explained how amnesia cases often had curious side-effects and how a whole imaginary picture could be conjured up by some simple chance remark overheard while in a susceptible state. He explained that he did some work at the general and might well have been spoken about on the wards.

How did the doctor account for the fact that he knew about Sister Charles, Peter asked in mounting frustration. 'She accompanies me, sometimes,' was the answer.

And the trousers? 'Lent by someone at the general.'

And the fact that the shop had burned down twenty years ago? 'That can't be right if they're new. You must have misread the label or been misled in the town.'

There was more, but the point was made – Peter had never been to that hospital, yet he recognized the doctor without being introduced and he knew how much change he needed for two cups of tea before he went into the café.

There is no doubt that Peter did disappear in full view of his guests, and that he walked into another dimension – an alternative universe – whatever name you choose. I stayed with the family over a weekend, and we went through the whole experience, together with some of the witnesses to the original vanishing. One of them actually saw it happen by reflection in the living-room window, so there is no mileage in the temporary blindness idea. The trousers that Peter borrowed were the lynch-pin of the whole matter, and he let me take them for independent examination. All tailoring marks are a matter of public record, and it was confirmed that the one on the corduroy slacks was genuine. I had asked for any information on the corduroy itself, and it was confirmed to be of recent manufacture. Interestingly, the zip was recognized as a new kind, in use only since 1968, fourteen years after the tailor's burned down.

The only possibility left, and it was a far-fetched one,

was that it was an old label sewn into a new pair of trousers. How and why *anyone* should want to keep a label spotless for fourteen years would have been a difficult question to answer, but I felt I owed it to the reader to ignore no possibility, however remote. The reply from the manufacturer was a curious one and a bonus for my zeal. It confirmed that the label had been fastened to the trousers in that firm's traditional way and that all stitching was theirs and had not been tampered with. They did ask for the address of the tailor whose name was on the label, however (having been unable to make contact themselves), explaining that the colour was not an exact match with their corduroys and asking if I knew what dye had been used to give them that special hint of green, as they would very much like to incorporate it into future production.

It is interesting that Peter recalls the ward 'shimmering', as if the two universes were still in a state of flux around him (as they must have been for him to return). The feeling he had of being slower of speech suggests an energy different between himself and the other dimension, a very consistent idea.

The contents of Peter's pockets subsequent to his return? One packet of Senior Service plain, with two cigarettes remaining: although these are from the other dimension, the coding on the cigarettes is normal for that region and time. One silk handkerchief with JB monogrammed on it. 27p in change: Peter thinks he had some loose silver in his jeans, passed on to him by a nurse at the time of his borrowing the trousers – some of the money was change from the other tea-room but was indistinguishable from our money.

Presumably there was a Peter in the other dimension, too. Since everything was so remarkably similar, it is more than likely that he was living in an almost identical house. Where was he during these events? There is no suggestion that any kind of 'swop' had taken place, so it is surely reasonable to suppose that – for a while – two Peters were existing in the same dimension. If that is so, it is surely a mercy for both of them that they didn't come face to face.

Miscellany IV:
Journey into Mystery

It is probably a particular vanity of every age to assume that it is special in some way. The late twentieth century, however, seems to have turned this mild eccentricity into an art-form!

People think it fashionable to talk about the 'stress of modern living', when science has eliminated most of the hard work, medicine has liberated us from the worst effects of disease, and social progress has removed the fear of workhouses and starvation. It is not Utopia, but if the parents of anyone over fifty were to come back as 20-year-olds, they might be forgiven for thinking that the millennium had arrived.

The other great delusion is that all strange phenomena are a product of this scientific era. It may help those who think this way to reflect on the reports we have of UFOs 'buzzing' the armies of Alexander the Great in the fourth century BC.

What is interesting is that what people see tends to be the product of the intellectual environment in which they live. During the Middle Ages, the time of great piety, it was flying monks and glowing Madonnas. In our scientific age, it is flying saucers and glowing extra-terrestrials. Then people were enchanted by fairies and carried off to never-never land, now they are hypnotized by alien rays and carried off in spaceships. On one level, therefore, nothing has changed: people will always be 'seeing things', and these will reflect their times. On the other hand, there are real things to be seen, and people see them in every age – our problem is to separate the gold from the dross and look for a common pattern. I now know that non-human beings, not of this world, walk about our planet, and probably have for thousands of years. I call them alien entities; my ancestors called them the Evil One or angels, depending on the circumstances prevailing.

The story of Lot in Genesis is a curious one, as is the story in the book of Ezekiel. In the first, two men come to warn Lot and his family that the city is about to be destroyed. How they know this must remain forever speculation, but they have a fairly exact knowledge of when it is going to happen, because they stay in the city all night. They use some sort of disorientation device on a lynch mob (the Bible says they blinded them, but the phrase '... so they wearied themselves to find the door' does not suggest physical blindness; blind men can find a door they are already standing outside, and men blinded in such a dramatic way do not hang around to find out what other horrors such powerful assailants have up their sleeves). The Lot family leave and are enjoined not to look back; Lot's wife does and is turned into a pillar of salt. If it were a damaged spaceship whose atomic engines were going to explode, not to look back at the appalling flash is good advice. If Lot's wife did not look back in the physical sense but returned because she couldn't bear to go out into the wilderness, she might well have been discovered later encased in salt. This phenomenon was observed in some cases after the bombs were dropped in Hiroshima and Nagasaki – people covered in a fairly thick coat of salt. The whole of the Lot story could have been a folktale, but the mention of a terrific explosion ('... the smoke of the country went up like the smoke of a furnace') *and* the pillar of salt (a phenomenon associated only with nuclear explosions) are somewhat of a coincidence, although one cannot put it higher than that.

Ezekiel would seem to have seen a spaceship – '... whirlwind came out of the north, a great cloud and a fire.' Four creatures emerge from this, and each has four faces: 'the face of a man and a face of a lion on the right, the face of an ox on the left, and also the face of an eagle'. A lyrical way of describing a space-traveller's helmet, perhaps. What lift this account above the run-of-the-mill fantasies of antiquity are the statements about the wheels the creatures wore. That is an odd thing to invent, especially as further details very much suggest that these were personal helicopter packs. I won't labour the point, but Ezekiel is at pains to stress that the wheels were the guiding power of these men ('... for the spirit of the living creatures was in the wheels') and that the wheels made a noise ('like the noise of great waters'), and on the creatures heads was glass – '... upon the heads of the living creatures was as the colour of the terrible crystal stretched over their heads above' (Ezekiel I, vv. 4–28).

Similar stories are encountered in other ancient writings. In one old Indian work, a light is shone through a ruby to destroy a distant mountain. Well, I have seen light passed through a ruby and blow a hole in a steel plate, only it was called a laser in my time.

These examples are probably endless and prove nothing, but they are food for thought.

On the evening of 8 January 1974 Richard Evans was idly watching his TV, waiting for his son to get back, so he could lock up and go to bed. The boy had been to see some friends in the next village and was due in, by strict rule, before ten. At ten past, the father became a little worried – the boy was an excellent timekeeper – and he decided to check with his son's friends. They said he had left at a quarter past nine, to have ample time for the journey.

It was a bitterly cold night, with severe iceing on the roads, so Mr Evans wondered if the buses had been cancelled or delayed, but there was a phone at the bus stop, and he knew that his son would have rung to let him know if anything was likely to have delayed him. The alternative was that he had walked across country, in which case he would be home by about half past ten. The father continued to half-look at the screen, half at his watch. At a quarter to eleven he was seriously alarmed and decided to check with the police.

A sudden flickering of the screen caught his attention, and as he looked, the picture wobbled and flickered, then went dead, leaving only a fuzzy glow. When he moved forward to switch it off, the screen came alive again. In black and white he saw a picture of the woods only a few hundred yards from his home, with a close-up of the pond the children used for sailing model boats. Its surface was a solid chunk of ice , except the far corner, which was black. The picture then went into close-up and, to his amazement, he saw his son lying unconscious on the bank, his legs in the freezing water. He rushed out and reached the pond in a few minutes. There, exactly as he had seen it on the TV, was his son. The boy had slipped and knocked himself out, and his falling legs had smashed the ice. Without the inexplicable TV appearance he could well have died from exposure.

A number of other people who had been watching the programme were questioned by the father, but all reported that everything had been normal.

Ted Serios* was able to project ideas onto film at very close range with strong concentration, but for a boy to cut out the power of a BBC transmitter and zoom in for a close-up, all while he was unconscious, is an astonishing feat.

To date, this phenomenon has never repeated itself, but a similar case is reported by Professor Hugo Smiles, from Brazil this time. In that case a whole family saw a daughter being raped and murdered – a horrific experience for them, its only saving grace being that the family were able to identify the murderers. This was not admissible evidence, of course, but it did allow the police to get a confession.

Michael Findlater was evacuated during the latter part of the war (1944) to a small village in Cornwall. Unbeknown to him, his father was killed on active service, and a flying bomb killed his mother when it crashed on their house in the East End of London. Most of the surrounding houses were either destroyed, damaged beyond repair or finished off by the resulting fire. His elder brother, then sixteen, had wandered off and disappeared from sight from then on.

---

* Ted Serios was an American phenomenon of the 1970s. He could project his thought-images onto film in cameras pointed at him. He has now slipped into obscurity.

When Michael returned at the end of the war, all his family and friends had either been killed, disappeared or moved from the dereliction of the bombing. He spent the rest of his childhood in a series of orphanages and generally had a miserable life. His one obsession was to find his brother, and he used to search the streets hoping to catch sight of him boarding a bus or catching a train, but all his efforts proved futile. When he was old enough to work, he spent a lot of his wages on advertising in various publications for his missing brother, but nothing came of that either.

Michael showed a natural gift for business and was soon a wealthy man, with offices in the West End. One morning he came to work and was told that his secretary had phoned in sick. Never one to let matters slide, he got her worksheet out, to do whatever she had booked. At the top of the list was a seven-figure number, with the name Bell written against it, and 'URGENT' in red ink. He dialled the number, a girl answered and he asked for Mr Bell. She replied that there was no Bell there that she knew of, although she was only a temp. Would he care to phone later, when Mr Findlater, the boss, would be there? Michael says he felt the skin on the back of his neck prickle as he asked, as casually as he could, 'Is that Harry Findlater?' The girl said that it was. 'With an owl tattooed on the back of his hand?' Yes. And the long separated brothers were together again.

When his secretary came back to work, he asked her who on earth had given her his brother's number. She looked at the worksheet. 'Oh, that's not a phone number. It's Mr Bell's bank account number [Lloyd's]. You asked me to get it for our credit check.' A million-to-one coincidence, or guidance from somewhere else?

Twenty-five years ago, when some excavations were being made under York Minster, one of our most glorious cathedrals, a young policeman remained there alone after the workmen had gone, checking something, as he was keenly interested in archaeology. Suddenly he heard the sound of a trumpet blast, and out of the flat wall, deep under this huge church, a party of Roman soldiers came marching. They were led by an officer on a horse and looked very dishevelled and miserable. They marched past into the other wall, quite oblivious of him. He was so terrified that he nearly fell off his ladder.

He was, however, more terrified of the reception he would get if he told the story, especially in the light of his job. As a result, he kept silent about it until he retired just a few years ago. When he did speak, he was surprised to find that many people had seen them over the years and that they are still regularly visible. (Visitors are advised to check with the Minster authorities to ascertain times of opening etc.)

The MacPhersons are a husband-and-wife team of doctors. The year was 1972 and they had been back to Scotland for a holiday together and, as they would have to return to work almost as soon as they arrived back, they decided to make the journey home as relaxing as possible. Accordingly, they drove during the night, stopping at their destination town long before the rush-hour began. They then went sightseeing during the morning, slept during the afternoon, had dinner and drove on again when the roads were once again almost empty.

They were on the last leg of their journey, and the time was just after two. Malcolm was about to take the right-hand fork in the road when a gesticulating figure caught their attention. He was a man in his late forties, dirty and dishevelled, and with bad cuts on his face. Malcolm is a rugby player and six feet four, so he had no qualms about stopping, even though the man resembled a desperate-looking tramp. The man stumbled up in the full glare of the headlights and pointed down the other part of the fork, a B-road. 'Crashed my car – need help – please drive me to a phone.' Explaining that they were doctors, Malcolm told him to get into the back, where his wife joined him, as he seemed to be in shock. She recalls taking his hand, which felt cold, but that is usual in such cases.

They rapidly reached the stricken vehicle, which had hit a tree. Inside were three people, the driver, a woman and a young child. All seemed unconscious. The doctors checked their pulses, to find the man dead and the other two in a bad way. They had difficulty reaching the injured child, as the driver, who was pinned tightly between the buckled steering-wheel and his seat, had trapped the boy's leg. They took the chance of removing both the survivors, as there was a dreadful reek of petrol and they feared that the car would catch fire at any moment. They were too engrossed in their work to notice until afterwards that the man who had summoned them was nowhere to be seen.

When they had done as much as they could, Malcolm stayed and Alison went to fetch the emergency services. The police, ambulance and fire brigade soon arrived, and the injured were removed to hospital. The car was drenched in foam, and the gruesome task of removing the body began. When that was completed, Malcolm was asked to make a formal examination. The man stretched out on the road was the same man who had flagged them down; there could be no doubt. Alison confirmed this, particularly remembering the odd-shaped cut on the back of the hand when she held it in the back of the car. The face had the same pattern of bruises and cuts, and the clothes were the same as they had seen when the man was illuminated in their headlights for the full five seconds it took him to reach the car. Had it not been for their timely arrival, both the mother and the child would have died and, somehow, the father had managed to look for help, although Malcolm would give evidence at the inquest that he had died instantly in the crash.

The story told by the MacPhersons is not an uncommon one. The reader may find this surprising, considering the implications of the incident, but such cases have been noted through the ages. What makes this one especially noteworthy is that we have two witnesses (ninety per cent of all paranormal happenings are experienced by a solitary person) and that they fulfil all the criteria psychic researchers look for in incidents of this kind.

The MacPhersons were used to acting coolly in an emergency, and the prospect of visiting a serious car crash did not fill them with panic and horror, as it would most of us. They were not tired or under the influence of any drugs or alcohol, and both saw the apparition clearly and for quite a length of time. Mrs MacPherson actually sat with him in the back of the car. They have no axe to grind, only telling me the story because they feel strongly that the subject of ghosts, life after death, and all the other things not normally acknowledged by professional people, should be treated as dispassionately and scientifically as any other phenomenon in the world.

The reader will have noticed that in all these reports, there have been either two or more witnesses, or physical evidence has remained afterwards to support the truth of the experience. I have no doubt that most solitary observations of inexplicable happenings are perfectly true, but I have been loath to include them in what is my first book. This is not because I doubt the integrity of my informants, far from it, but we can all mistake what we see, or certain physical conditions, both from inside the observer and externally, can distort our perception of reality. For example, there is a disease that attacks some kinds of wheat, called Ergot. Modern farming and health regulations have almost eradicated it, but in times past it used to infect bread and cause the most frightful hallucinations. It is possible that other substances may have a similar, although milder effect on people quite without their knowledge, so I have generally concentrated on the group-experience, particularly where units of that group were members of society not given to imagining things or being carried away by mass emotion. For instance, soldiers, policemen and doctors.

The next case raises questions much more profound than the simple 'is there life after death?' (as do so many), and I include it because there were over sixty people present at the happening, including members of the groups mentioned above. Those I have met seem a level-headed bunch of people, especially the Spiritualists. Some readers will find that a curious remark, and I hasten to explain. I am not a Spiritualist, although I agree with a lot that they say and have always found theirs a most reasonable movement. The popular prejudice is, however, the reverse.

There are two sorts of people interested in psychic phenomena. The first is the seeker after truth who is more ruthless in rooting out fraud among his own than any outsider could ever be. He or she is the Spiritualist with the capital 'S', and I would think I had much more chance of pulling the wool over the eyes of the average scientist than I would one of this group. The second sort is the thrill-seeker, the person who loves to be duped. They are common enough in any movement and give the public a jaundiced view of whatever they latch onto, whether it be Socialism or Spiritualism.

Michael Trevillion had been a lifelong Spiritualist and a successful businessman, a doer of good by stealth, and a bitter enemy of the corrupt side of his cherished movement. To his irritation, he came briefly into the public eye when, just after the war, he exposed a group of fraudulent mediums in East London preying on those who had lost loved-ones. (An amusing side of this was how it put the judiciary and the newspapers in a cleft stick. Both were implacable foes of Spiritualism, yet here was a self-confessed member of the detested group on the side of the angels.)

On his death in 1975, a select group returned to the family home after the service. There were representatives of Spiritualist organizations worldwide, business colleagues and men and women Michael Trevillion had made friends of during a long and useful life. A brief list of the positions of the more prominent guests will assure the reader that what was seen cannot be doubted on the grounds of unreliable witnesses: the deputy lord lieutenant of the county, a detective chief superintendent, two QCs, a knighted surgeon, three senior representatives of the national press and a circuit judge. There were also a number of City financiers. Among the women were two BBC editors and a columnist whose name is a household word.

The time was just approaching four, and the dull November day had almost become night when the widow, Martha, herself a noted Spiritualist and author, rose to say a few words. She and Michael had, she said, promised to try to give some sign that they had survived death, and it had been agreed long before that this manifestation should be attempted at four on the afternoon of the funeral. This, she explained, was a secret known only to the two of them, and she had waited until only a few minutes before the allotted time, to allow no one the opportunity of contriving something, from either malicious or compassionate motives. She had timed her speech to perfection, and when she sat down there were only seconds left. Those I spoke to say that the atmosphere was very highly charged. All knew the couple, and many had had psychic experiences and messages as a result of attending seances run by these two remarkable people.

As the chimes of four began, there occurred something that changed the lives of many of those present and left an indelible impression on everyone. The room was suddenly filled with the most overpowering fragrance of flowers, and fresh primroses fell from nowhere in great profusion, covering furniture and people alike. As this rain of flowers continued, the unmistakable strains of 'Amazing Grace' (Martha's favourite hymn) could be heard quite clearly, coming from the centre of the room. After about a minute the fall stopped. Many of the guests were sobbing unashamedly, but the mood was one of happiness and joy, not sorrow.

Of all those I have spoken to, no one doubts that everything was authentic. Not only would it be impossible to fake such a demonstration, but it would have been unthinkable to anyone who knew Martha even to imagine the idea crossing her mind. Likewise, and much more telling from a scientific researcher's standpoint, primroses could not be acquired anywhere in the world at that time (perhaps why there were sent, since they had no special significance to either Martha or Michael).

There is a curious footnote to this beautiful and moving story, and concerns the primroses growing in the woods which form part of the estate. The next spring when they were in full bloom, Martha made daily trips to admire the beauty of her flowers and to marvel at the wonderful events of the winter. The primroses carpeted the ground in great profusion and were at the peak of their glory when she saw them for the last time. The next morning, when she made her customary journey, not a solitary bloom remained.

Was it possible that Michael's spirit was able to move forward in time and pick primroses at the height of their beauty? If not, where *did* they come from?

Martha died in 1988. She lies next to Michael in the lovely village churchyard, their graves covered in a sea of primrose plants, so that every spring certain visitors will be reminded of the miracle they were privileged to witness on that bleak November afternoon.

FAMILY

The Ring that Refuses to Stay Lost

There are many astonishing stories in this book, and with some we are hard-pressed even to guess at a solution. In this case, however, there seems *nothing* to come to grips with. It is not a visitation from beyond the grave, nor can it be a fantastic coincidence. The two subsequent incidents I shall report are odd in themselves, although mere bagatelle compared to the primary story, yet they cast an even more impenetrable fog around the whole thing. There is something decidedly peculiar going on, but we cannot even get a toehold on the foothills of this amazing occurrence.

John Scott's life has been devoted to serving mankind in general, with his medical work, and his fellow-countrymen in particular, with his duties as soldier and ambassador.

He can trace his mother's family back to the fourteenth century, when the first members arrived from Moravia (now in Czechoslovakia). 'Moravia' has become corrupted to 'Murray' and is the name of one of the principal actors in this uncanny tale, who in 1855 went with the British Army to the Crimea, where he lost a fob-seal bearing the family coat of arms. This seemingly brief and unremarkable biography is misleading, because it sets in motion a train of events that would subsequently baffle some of the clearest minds of John Scott's generation.

In the tradition of his father's family, John was commissioned into the Argyll and Sutherland Highlanders, and he was eventually posted to what is now Israel, in the Airborne Division. It was this body, together with the Palestine Police, that eventually bore the brunt of the guerrilla war with Jewish nationalists fighting for a homeland. As a lieutenant, John had nothing to do with high policy and had only his military duties to consider.

In February 1946 he had a motor-cycle accident and was confined to hospital for some months. One night he had the most peculiar dream. In it, his mother (who was still very much alive) appeared in the city of Nablus, the capital of Samaria, a place John had merely passed on his way to Jerusalem. In the dream his mother was walking along the main street, turning right, then left, then right again and into a narrow lane, at the end of which she disappeared.

As soon as he was sufficiently fit again, John got his driver to take him to Nablus. There he found the streets his mother had walked along in his dream, and he followed her path on foot. The memory of his dream was still so vivid that he had no difficulty in recognizing the various streets through which she had passed. Eventually he arrived at the cul-de-sac which had been the final part of her journey. He was forced to stop at the end of the road, which contained a small bazaar. While he waited to see what would happen, he glanced idly at the gew-gaws and ornaments an Arab was holding on a tray suspended by a string from his neck. He doesn't know why but he took what appeared to be a red button that was lying among the hundreds of trinkets on the tray (it was the first and only thing he picked up). Idly he turned it over – and received a tremendous shock: on it were engraved a mermaid and the words 'Tout Prest' ('Quite Ready'), the crest and the motto of his own family. Considerably surprised, he bought the item and kept it until his next leave.

Back home, his grandmother recognized it as a fob-seal, one of a pair (the other being at the ancestral home in Scotland). It was, she said, undoubtedly genuine. The reason she could be so sure is, in itself, curious. While the true crest showed the mermaid holding a glass in her right hand and a comb in the left, the craftsman who had made the two fob-seals had forgotten that the image of his die would be reversed and that the resulting imprint would show the mermaid with a comb in the right hand, the glass in the left. This made them unique. The then Captain (later Colonel) John Murray, John Scott's great-uncle, had taken one of these seals with him to the Crimea, and it had been lost there during his period of service (1855–6) with the Grenadier Guards.

John Scott had the seal mounted as a ring and wore it constantly. On one occasion, when he was crewing in a yacht race, his fingers had shrunk under the effect of the cold water and, as he moved forward quickly to catch something, the ring flew from his finger, straight towards the ocean and perpetual loss. By chance (?) it struck the thin length of wire that stretched itself around the boat, and bounced back to safety. This wire was less than a quarter of an inch thick, yet the ring had hit that one spot out of all the myriad other places it could have gone, and had been almost miraculously restored to its owner.

When John returned to Cambridge after the war to complete his studies, he came back from a party, a little merry perhaps, and contrived to leave the ring in the washroom of his college. In the morning, distraught, he hunted high and low, asked porters and staff, but of the ring there had been no word. That night he had another dream, of a door with the staircase number E5 on it, and he knew that his ring was there. In the morning he made his way to this room and asked the student occupant if he had found the ring. Much surprised, the student produced the ring and asked if it was the one. He had had to leave the college early on the day he found it, and had returned only that morning, and would have handed it into the porter's lodge on his way to his first lecture. He had told no one of his discovery of the ring and, in fact, had given it scant thought, assuming it to be a piece of costume jewellery of little value.

To date (1989) John and his ring have never been accidentally parted, and I don't think they could be, even if he tried!

When we reflect on the strangeness of the events that led a man to be guided by the vision of his still-living mother to the place in the whole of the Middle East where his ancestor's fob-seal was for sale, we must confess ourselves at a complete loss for a rational explanation.

The story was thoroughly investigated by the Psychical Research Society, but if they have reached any conclusions, John has not been informed.

The Flower Child

My next story concerns a wealthy lady, a renowned scholar and author. We have sadness and mystery, but it is a hopeful story, although it must make us reflect on the true nature of the human spirit when it survives death, if there is a consistency at all.

The lady of this report (1959), although titled, we shall refer to as Jane Smith. She had a beautiful cottage left to her by her mother in Dorset but was unable to take up residence until she retired a few years later. In the meantime, on her mother's recommendation she allowed a lady from the nearby village to live in it rent-free in return for maintaining the house and gardens. She made odd visits during her holidays and found the woman and her work very satisfactory.

To say that Jane Smith 'retired' is to say that she left her position as lecturer at a university but, as with so many people in her position, her workload increased, so that when she announced her intention of taking up full-time occupancy, she offered the woman the job of house-keeper. She did this partly because she needed one, and partly because she had no wish to deprive her of what must have seemed to be her home. The woman thanked her but explained that she had a long-standing invitation to share a property with a sister in Essex, which she intended to take up.

Jane Smith then took up the place. She was rather surprised to find that she couldn't get a replacement for her old housekeeper, even though she offered good wages. Being a practical woman of simple wants, she took to fending for herself. Her writing she posted off to be typed, the tradesmen provided her with all she needed, and she had fun learning the simpler skills of cookery. Her only worry was the garden, for a gardener was likewise unobtainable; the garden was mercifully small, so she did the same as with the housekeeping, and got by admirably.

Jane did ask some of the tradesmen why she could get no staff, and they became uneasy and embarrassed. She began to wonder if her views on society, and especially those relating to the lack of purpose of marriage except for the rearing of children, had been noised abroad. She was radical in her opinions about the position of women in a social and sexual sense and would have been called an exponent of 'free-love' in earlier times. It was unlikely that these views had percolated to this fairly isolated village, but there seemed no other way to explain the curious behaviour of the locals. Jane's mother had been a resident since childhood, only leaving to marry. Before any action could be taken to sell the cottage, the Smiths had inexplicably fallen out, and the young wife, had returned to spend the rest of her days in self-inflicted celibacy and solitude. Jane had been born in a nursing home in London, returning to Dorset only for holiday visits, spending most of her time at her father's home and seeing her mother at arranged times. This is a common enough thing these days, but then it was all considered rather odd and slightly improper. Jane often reflects that this is the cause of her never marrying and her holding strong views on women's freedom in and out of marriage.

A month or six weeks after she had moved in, she answered a knock at the door. A very pretty little girl was standing there, and she asked if she might come from time to time to play in the garden and sometimes to pick some flowers. Jane was more than happy to agree, and the little girl came and went as she pleased. Sometimes she took flowers, never many, and walked home with them right away.

As time went by, Jane became more and more curious. Christine, as she had learnt the girl's name was, always wore the same dress, and it was always spotlessly clean, as if she had a whole wardrobe full of identical clothes. The other odd thing was the behaviour of the visiting tradesmen. Although the girl was plainly visible, they never commented on her, and Jane felt it beneath her dignity, as well as an oblique affront to the child, to ask them anything about her behind her back, as it were.

When Christine did come inside the house – and this was rare, despite Jane's repeated invitations – she behaved as though she were familiar with the whole layout. She never stayed long, seeming to prefer the garden. As winter came, the little girl's visits continued in exactly the same way, and Jane was most concerned. She would play in her ordinary dress whatever the temperature and seemed oblivious to the cold. By this time Jane was seriously anxious. The girl looked well fed and well turned-out, yet she had no warm clothing. On Jane's next visit to the village, mystification greeted her enquiries. People were adamant that no such child lived in or around the village, and suggested she might be a gypsy girl, as these people passed through from time to time. This was most unsatisfactory, as there was no gypsy camp for miles.

The next day when Christine came and picked a small bunch of chrysanthemums, Jane decided to follow her home. The little girl skipped away in her usual fashion, and a guilty but determined Jane followed discreetly. The child went down the lane, crossed a small road and walked up the turning that led to the vicarage. Feeling despicable, Jane hopped from tree to tree, keeping her tiny quarry in sight. Christine turned off the road and walked among the tombstones. She stopped at one and matter-of-factly placed the flowers on the grave, then turned to move out of Jane's sight. She followed, but the search was in vain: the great monumental marbles and the trees and bushes made the cemetery a virtual maze. Nevertheless she continued her search until darkness made it impossible and futile to continue. The child would long have been at home by her warm fire while she, Jane, stumbled about among frosty graves.

The lack of success did not daunt her, and she determined to be closer to the child when next she followed her. That occurred four days later, and by this time Jane was better prepared: she had soft but hardy shoes and a powerful torch and had made herself feel ludicrous by blacking her face and wearing dark clothes. As Christine skipped off, Jane was after her with a will, keeping much closer this time.

The routine was performed as before, but this time Jane had got to a position of advantage as the child approached. Realizing that she might need her torch, the evening having grown suddenly dark, she groped in her pocket for it, catching her sleeve on a protruding stump and losing her footing. This sent her staggering out in full view of the little girl. Christine seemed quite unperturbed and placed the flowers as before, then turned to say hello. Jane found her breath.

'I didn't mean to spy on you, my dear, but I was so worried about you – whether you were being properly looked after at home.'

The girl smiled. 'Don't worry about me.'

Jane moved towards her. 'But what are you doing out in all weathers in this horrible place?'

The girl seemed surprised at the question. 'Mummy always came here in the evening, and now I must – for a little while.'

Jane remembers feeling uneasy as she asked her next question: 'Who was your mummy?'

'The lady who lived at your house. Didn't you know her?'

Jane was now quite confused. 'But your mummy has gone away. Why aren't you with her? Do you want me to telephone her for you, or the police?'

The little girl smiled again. 'No, thank you. You can't, and please don't worry. If I worry you, I won't come again.' This was said kindly, with no threat implied.

Jane had not realized how fond she had become of the young girl who had all but adopted her, and the words gushed out: 'Oh, don't do that. Come and live with me if you want to, but don't go away, please.'

The little girl tilted her head as if listening, then she turned back to Jane. 'I can come once more, in the spring. Goodbye till then, and *please* don't worry. I'm very happy.' Then she simply turned and walked away – not rudely but as if she had been called, and she was soon swallowed up in the darkness.

Jane has no idea how long she stood there until she switched the torch on to light the gravestone with the tiny bunch of flowers as its base. The inscription was a simple one. 'Sacred to the Memory of Christine Sinclair, beloved daughter of Amy. 1889–1898. Sorely missed.'

Jane's mother's maiden name was Amy Sinclair, and

she had married Jane's father, a titled man, in early 1896, Jane being born in the November of the same year.

Jane then did something she had sworn she would never do: she read her mother's youthful diaries, still preserved immaculately among her effects. They confirmed that Christine was illegitimate and she, Amy, deserted by the father. She had sent the child away to avoid her life being made a misery in the village, and had married in the hope of providing her beloved Christine with a name and perhaps an inheritance. Jane's father, perhaps not unreasonably, had flown into a terrible rage at being told the facts and being asked for his blessing on what he saw as a shameful act, and the marriage had ended in separation, but not divorce. Christine had died of scarlet fever and had been brought back for burial in her native village with the permission of a kindly vicar. Jane's mother had never breathed a word to anybody.

Pressed into the diary was a withered daffodil with a small card on which was written in a childish hand, 'With love to Mummy'.

Jane was not religious and took an agnostic view of the world, but during the coming bleak months she prayed for Christine and for her mother. Not prayers to anyone recognized by the orthodox faiths but to the force she now believed brought an inexplicable order to the universe.

The conclusion of this story is the most moving thing I have ever heard. On 15 April Jane awoke with a start and a feeling that something momentous was going to happen. Running to the window, she looked out at her spring garden. At the gate was Christine, waving what seemed to be a farewell and pointing towards the front door. When Jane reached it and had it open, Christine was no longer there, but lying serenely on the flagstones was a solitary daffodil.

Reincarnation

Of all the mysteries we face, reincarnation is both the most exciting and the hardest to get certain evidence about. The idea that each soul goes on through life after life, gradually learning from its mistakes, eventually to arrive at a perfect state, fascinates us all.

The great problem with all evidence of reincarnation is eliminating the possibility that the person who is the supposed rebirth of someone else did not get their information by a perfectly normal method. The further trouble with all this is that the people concerned are almost invariably honest. I spent some time talking to a fellow who thought he had been born a Frenchman in a previous life. He had had no formal French teaching at school and was a duffer at languages; so it was difficult to explain his facility with a lot of French idioms. It was only thanks to a chance remark from his sister that I discovered that the family had had a number of French au-pairs long before he was old enough to remember. Unfortunately, this is true in so many cases, and one doesn't feel like expending the considerable research effort for so dubious a result.

The most convincing story I know of, and one where it seems most unlikely that the reborn one could know anything at all about her previous life, was told to me by a police officer. It was in the early 1950s and he was a young constable, married with no children. At that time he had a desk job which he found very irksome, so one beautiful afternoon, with his wife away, he decided to walk to the station. It was a good hike through the East End of London over to the West End, but he gave himself ample time and set out. As he reached the most run-down part of the district, a large Cockney lady, one with a genuine heart of gold, summoned him with that regal authority that seems to be an inborn feature of such ladies. She had with her a scruffy, ill-dressed child of about five, typical of those post-war times of austerity. The girl was lost – or so it seemed, and since the lady had not the resources in time or food to care for the child, she demanded that the authorities do something. They being represented by my friend, he took charge of the little waif, determined to take her to his station where she could be given the good meal she so obviously needed.

The girl put her finger resolutely in her mouth and declined to say a word. After a time she became tired and bored, so he carried her. She didn't weigh much, although she did not seem to be in especially poor condition for the age and area in which she lived. From her coign of vantage she looked round at the new places there were coming into view. To her, no doubt, a ride on a policeman's shoulder was a high treat.

They had travelled about three miles like that and moved into an area of better-class property, much of it still in ruins, when she suddenly seemed to become very agitated and began pointing at the shell of a building that stood on a corner. There was not much of it left, and the boards that had been put up to keep trespassers out had themselves been stolen for fuel. She was not to be placated and kept saying, 'I lived there.' She was neither the right age nor of the right background for the story to be plausible, so my friend continued with his tiny burden. But she wouldn't have it. Kicking and struggling, she forced him to put her down, upon which she ran across to the almost demolished building. It still had a substantial shell, although a large part of the roof had been blown away, and was obviously quite safe. As he still had plenty of time, he decided to humour her, asking when it was that she had lived there. She seemed not to hear and just stood staring fixedly at the façade of the house.

'This used to be Brickfields, you know,' she said, and a strange feeling came over my friend. It was still the voice of a little girl, but the whole manner was of an adult. She stood up quite straight, and her features changed from the fractious grimaces of the young child to the self-possession of a grown woman. 'This all has a purpose, Constable. I hope you realize that?'

He remembers gazing open-mouthed at her. 'What has a purpose, Madam?' (He is anxious to make the point clear that he called her 'madam' because she was speaking like a mature person.)

'It means that I've been given a chance to do something that I was prevented from doing last time, and I feel I must hurry – I don't think I shall be back long.'

He remembers feeling that events were getting out of hand for a police officer of twenty-two, and he fell back on his authority. 'I don't know what all this means, but you'd better come with me to the station and talk it over with the sergeant.' (He recalls those as the most embarrassing words he ever has to remember.)

She shook off his hand with impatience. 'I shall only be a few minutes, and I need your help.'

His resistance was at an end: the firmness in the voice coming from the little girl did not give him a choice. Pointing the way, she got him to force his way through a hole in the wall and to lead her down some old stone steps into a cellar. From behind a brick she extracted a small case; in it were some letters. She handed them to him.

'I wrote these before, but I never posted them. They will explain so much to him. Will you promise me that you'll post them?'

He nodded and promised. 'Can you explain what is going on?' he asked.

She shook her head, the weariness of the little girl creeping back over her. 'I suppose I died in whatever it was that wrecked this house – droning noise, shouting from the street – remember your promise.'

A few seconds later the tired tones of the little girl were back, whining at him for bringing her to a filthy place crawling with spiders. He took her out, they fed and washed her at the station, and the tiny sleeping form was collected later by a frantic mother.

He put the letters, unread, into a big manila envelope and posted them on his way out next morning, and he remains convinced that he took a small part in some very strange but very important work that afternoon. To satisfy his own curiosity, he checked on the house. It had never had anything so vulgar as a formal plaque on it, but the older residents still remember that it was known as Brickfields.

Both as a policeman and as a normal human being, my

friend was not satisfied with this and wanted to find more. He had at his fingertips all the knowledge of a well-policed country that had been collecting information on its citizens for more than twelve years and which had everyone tagged by the identity card system.

His first call, was on the little girl, whom he now knew as Pamela, and her family. Her father and mother were respectable people, both aged twenty-four. The father had a relatively good job in a local printer's, and the mother worked assembling components for the radio industry. He brought Pamela small tokens of affection, such as sweets and the occasional cake, but never enough to make the hated word 'charity' come to their minds. He had become fond of the child, and it was not difficult to talk to the mother about herself and the little girl.

In those days the poor never travelled in the sense we understand it: a trip to the local market or a music hall half a mile down the road, or to the pub, was the maximum most people ever went in their lives. Holidays were still unknown in the going-away-for-a-holiday sense, and there was very little money about. When my friend asked about the neighbourhood in which Pamela had 'found' her old home, the woman had barely heard of it. It was 'up West', where the rich lived, and it neither interested her nor attracted her. She had never been a servant like many similarly placed girls, and had worked at the job she had now since she left school. It was the same for her husband. They were the typical East Londoners of their day: they knew the area they lived in, but a mile up the road was alien territory.

Satisfied that Pamela could not even have come across Brickfields by chance (even if she had, how could she have gone straight to the letters?), he turned his attention to its late tenants. Scotland Yard's files supplied him with all the information he needed after a search that lasted no more than an hour.

Mrs Amanda Philipps had been the lady of the house, married to a well-off barrister much her senior. A chat with some of the older officers at the station that served the Brickfields area told him that Philipps had been a familiar figure at what were then called the police courts.

He used to take a small number of cases for those who could not afford legal representation. Nothing was known about his wife, which was only to be expected. There was, however, a sister, two years younger, who now lived in North London.

She was a problem, because you can't go and say you think someone's sister has come back in the body of an East End child and expect to get taken seriously, even if you are a policeman. Taking a terrible chance with his career, he went and explained that he was trying to trace his mother's family and that her family name had come up. The woman, somewhat bohemian in manners and appearance, was most helpful. After a few meetings, he casually mentioned the name on the envelopes her 'sister' had given him to post. Surprisingly, she was quite open about it, assuming that he knew most of it already. (It is, of course, a standard police ruse to pretend to be better informed than one is, in order to get the subject to talk more freely.)

It emerged that Amanda, unhappy in her marriage, had fallen in love with a young RAF officer, and the affaire had greatly upset the family. A conference had been called, and it had been put to Amanda that her liaison with this young man would bring only discredit on a family which contained such luminaries as a bishop and a judge. With startling lack of selfishness, Amanda had written the young man a cold letter, severing the relationship completely, affirming that she no longer cared for him and would hold it a great favour if he made no effort to see her again. The lady he was speaking to, May, had been the sole dissenting voice in this great family council but, as she was Amanda's junior, had no profession and lacked a powerful husband to back her up, she was totally ignored. All she could be was Amanda's confidante, consoling her wretched sister during a very bitter period. Amanda used to write letters to this officer, explaining the pressures exerted on her and begging his forgiveness. Despite May's urging, however, she could never be persuaded to send them. She had given her word to the family, she said, and that was not something that she could break. Her misery was soon to come to an end, as a lone German bomber, off course from the docks, flattened the house. Amanda and her husband were both killed, and May had the unenviable task of informing the young man. He was, of course, heartbroken but there was nothing to be done, and life went on. May had never married and had used her inheritance to fund her hobby of painting.

My friend had by then come to have a pretty shrewd idea of the calibre of this woman and risked all by telling her the true story. She was flabbergasted and delighted, reincarnation being one of those things that was 'in' with the set she was with. She naturally wanted to meet the girl, but my friend was becoming more and more anxious and self-reproachful. What had started out as a straightforward investigation into a strange happening was drawing him deeper into a web. He had already been deceitful with May and Pamela's mother, not to mention improper use of confidential files, and now he was being asked to put two people into a situation whose results he could not foresee, although he was well aware that the happiness of everyone, including his wife and himself, could be put in jeopardy by his obsession. But he was already in too deep. May was, naturally, quite insistent that she see the girl, and there seemed little he could do to prevent it, save refuse outright to co-operate, which would be too unfair to be considered. He made May promise to do nothing on her own initiative, and to respond only in kind to any reaction from Pamela. May was to pretend to be his elder sister, who had just happened to be passing, and they were to play it by ear from then.

Pamela was playing in the street when they arrived, and she gave May one of her head-on-the-side looks that my friend found so fetching. May was quite white and tense, and he himself was feeling slightly sick. Then more than he had dared to hope for happened. The far-away look came into the little child's eyes, and she whispered, 'Oh, my dear May, how lovely it is to see you again.' May knelt on the muddy pavement and embraced the child, and he walked away to leave them in private for what he was sure would be only a brief conversation. It lasted no more than a minute, but May was radiant; 'It was her – she said things only we knew – she went so quickly, but it was so beautiful.'

Perhaps it would have been a good thing if May and Amanda could have met again, and more been revealed, but it wasn't to be. Little Pamela died under the wheels of a bus only a few days later. May was inconsolable, and she retreated totally into herself, dying shortly afterwards. Whether there is any significance in the voice of Amanda being silenced, or whether it was chance, I cannot tell, but it is one of the most evidential cases for reincarnation that I know of.

In all the years that have elapsed since these events, my friend has found it impossible to forgive himself, and bitterly regrets that his curiosity led to such unhappy results. And that, I suspect, is the only meaningful tragedy in the whole story.

PROPHECY

Surrey's Mother Shipton

Alice Knight was born in 1923 in a small village near Guildford in Surrey. Her gifts of prophecy seem to have started when she was fifteen and have continued unabated until the present day. As with many seers, great events seem to have been the trigger that released her powers, but she has had many visions that dealt with local and mundane things.

In February 1938 she had the first prophetic dream she can remember, and it is noteworthy not only for its content but for the roundabout way her unconscious mind dealt with the information. She dreamt that she was watching what seemed to be a Pathé newsreel which showed a plane coming in to land. The commentator said: 'We are now ready to welcome home Mr Chamberlain, the Prime Minister, after his historic visit to see the German Chancellor, Herr Hitler.' The plane came to a stop, and the voice continued: 'We understand that Herr Hitler bet £5 that the British Prime Minister would take some action over Czechoslovakia, and Mr Chamberlain bet him £5 that he wouldn't – in a few minutes we shall know the result.' The plane door opened and Mr Chamberlain emerged, triumphantly waving a large white £5 note, and the dream stopped. She told her family of this because she thought it funny, not because she saw any political significance in it. In September, she was stunned to see her dream played out for real – almost – at Hendon, when Chamberlain returned with his famous piece of paper and 'peace for our time' speech. The humorous content of the dream had revealed a profound truth, and Chamberlain had in fact 'done nothing about Czechoslovakia'. Those who have seen archive pictures of the return will be struck by the similarity the notorious piece of paper bears to one of the old large white £5 notes.

In the meantime, Alice had had another very forceful dream, once again in the form of a newsreel. This was a collection of warlike incidents, men marching, tank battles, bombing raids etc, which was unremarkable in itself, as much newsreel footage was always devoted to the troubles around the world and there was no shortage of violent film. What was remarkable was that the end of the showing was marked by four numbers being superimposed onto the screen over the battles. The figures were 3939, and Alice was convinced that they meant that war would begin on 3 September 1939. She mentioned this to a number of people long before the event and became a minor celebrity when the dreadful happening material-ized on the day she had predicted.

By no means all Alice's visions have been so dramatic but, if anything, their commonplace content makes them all the more remarkable. One particular incident, well remembered by the surviving members of the family, occurred when she was home for a weekend leave from WRAF training. 'Somebody is going to lose a jewel, and they must look for it in a cabbage,' she said, but she was unable to expand on the statement, for it had just popped into her head without warning and without additional information. Her younger brother recalls that he came home from school later that week to find their next-door neighbour in the house, in tears. The stone (he thinks it was an opal) had come out of her engagement ring and was nowhere to be found. He reminded his mother of Alice's words, and the woman brightened. She explained that she had had some problems hanging out the washing, and she had fixed a temporary line up over the vegetable patch. All three went next door to the garden, and the woman threw her pinafore onto the ground and, despite the wartime food-shortage, pulled up cabbage after cabbage and shook them over the cloth. It was the sixth or seventh one that yielded the stone. The grateful woman showered the Knights with the vegetable, so that the brother recalls that they lived on boiled cabbage and bubble-and-squeak for what seemed like a month.

Alice explains that all her predictions are based either on dreams or on a sudden idea coming into her head with no background information whatsoever. Sometimes these visions relate to a particular person, but generally they are simply statements which future events must link to a particular person. An example of the former occurred on her WRAF station when she had the very strong feeling that a tyre was going to burst on the commandant's car. She was so obviously sincere that the woman took another vehicle. The technical officer, unaware of this, took the car herself a little later and escaped serious injury only by luck when the tyre burst and the car careered off the road and struck a tree. Because of this and other incidents, trivial in themselves, Alice acquired a reputation in the camp, and people started to come to her for advice before embarking on anything out of the ordinary. Without her mysterious prompter, her advice was no better than anyone else's, but she is a sensible and level-headed woman, and the advice she gave was plain commonsense and was right much more often than it was wrong. However, when strangers started to write seeking counsel, the CO advised her to apply for a posting where she wasn't known and to take the advice that was urged on posters all over the country, 'Keep it under your hat!' She thus survived the war without being driven mad by requests for help.

After the war Alice took a job with a local builder's merchants as secretary to the owner. With war-damage work and extensive rebuilding programmes, the times were good for the construction trade, and also seemed to see a flowering of Alice's special gift. The most significant of these glimpses was when one of their clients was about to demolish some damaged factory chimneys and had invited a select group of his friends to witness the spectacular event. On the way to the site, Alice had a glimpse of a future in which the explosives misfired and the chimney fell on some slum houses also due for demolition but occupied at that time by squatters. Her employer, who had had experience of her second-sight, insisted that the squatters be cleared. The site manager flatly refused, insisting that he had himself checked all the charges and was certain that all would go according to plan. So certain of Alice's abilities was her employer, however, that he parked his car with himself at the wheel in front of the houses and refused to go until the residents had been moved. In the event, the explosives did not malfunction, and he and Alice had to take a lot of banter from the other guests. On arriving back at the office they were informed that another demolition job, a few miles further in towards London, had gone tragically wrong, and a collapsing chimney had destroyed a row of houses, with terrible loss of life. Rightly or wrongly, this convinced her that her powers were too imprecise to be of any real use, she made a firm resolution never to tell anyone about her visions again.

This turned out to be a promise she could not keep, for sometimes the information in her dreams or visions was so unequivocal that she *had* to pass it on. A committed Socialist, she wrote to Clement Attlee to warn him against 'going to the country' again in 1951, predicting exactly how many seats the Conservatives would win by. She still has, as a treasured possession, the Labour leader's courteous but negative reply. On another occasion, when staying with friends at the seaside, she dreamt that a huge black wave rushed into her room and carried her out along the bed of a railway line. It was not water but a black sort of half-solid ooze, and it carried her past many stations with impossible names. It stopped at last at a station called Aberfan. She had never heard of the place, if it existed at all, and the lady of the house was Welsh and she had never heard of it. It was during the afternoon that followed the dream that a horrified country learnt of the great coal landslide that engulfed Aberfan school, killing numerous children. It was the first dream of this kind she had ever had, and she found it deeply upsetting. She began to suffer from depression as a result of guilt. She reasoned that, if she had not rejected the gift bestowed upon her, she might have examined the dream further and been able to do something to warn the inhabitants of the village.

To put her strange power to its best use, she took to sleeping with a tape-recorder by the side of the bed. One feature of the prediction dreams was that she always awakened after them, and she took to making notes while things were fresh in her mind. She had, she tells me, become very blasé about the visions and had often simply turned over and gone back to sleep, forgetting much significant detail by the morning. Now she endeavoured to extract as much information from them as possible and to pass it on to those involved. Much of her work she still keeps a secret, because, she says, some of the things have not happened or are in the process of being dealt with. As she has become older, the gift seems to be growing stronger, and the time-scale it works on is increasing. Before, events she foresaw generally took place within a few days; some, like the circumstances connected with World War II, were a year or so before their time, but she thinks that this was simply because of the sheer magnitude of what was going to happen. Now she sees things that are not due to take place until the twenty-first century, and few world leaders have not heard from her at some time or the other. She admits that often her warnings are ignored – her letter to President Reagan foreseeing the Challenger disaster received only a formal acknowledgement and, although she had a premonition of a nuclear accident in the Soviet Union, her lack of precise detail made it futile to alert the Soviet authorities.

Nevertheless, her record is a most impressive one, and it is quite impossible to make out a case that these predictions are just generalized guesses, some of which must come true on a statistical basis. She has diary after diary filled with incidents she has foreseen, with follow-up details of what actually occurred. Her predictions are not always correct, and some fail to materialize at all in the form that she has seen them; for all that, she has a success rate of about ninety-five per cent. Where the power comes from, she has no idea, although she remains convinced that God, or whatever force causes it, is doing it with a purpose. All her letters warning individuals, companies or nations contain a firm statement that she will accept nothing in return for her help. Frequently she does receive gifts from grateful people or firms, and she has been offered decorations from countries she has advised. She resolutely returns gifts and declines honours and, where no problems will result, she prefers to write her warnings anonymously.

She has allowed me to take notes of some of her long-range predictions, but only where they are of a general nature.

Despite President Bush's announcement to the contrary, the USA and the Soviet Union will come to an agreement for a joint expedition to Mars in 1993.

A cure for AIDS will become available in May 1992.

The EEC will ban all further Japanese investment in Europe by 1995.

Mrs Thatcher and the Conservative Party will win the next general election.

In 1990 President Gorbachev will use mounting unrest in the USSR to purge the Communist Party of the last of the hard-line conservatives.

The Catholic Church will face bankruptcy during 1997, and sweeping reforms will have to be made, which will include much closer links with the wealthy Nonconformist Churches of the United States.

The Voice

Albert Tanner is a very wealthy and respected man. Much of this is due to his many natural gifts but, as he himself insists, he would probably have a great deal less had it not been for his inseparable companion for the past thirty years. This guide and mentor comes in the form of a 'voice' which speaks to him from time to time. He describes it as a low whisper that seems to be coming into his left ear. The voice does not seem to have an emotional dimension to it, although it is not cold or aloof. It speaks to him as a man might tell him the time – an act of common politeness but with no especial significance.

This extraordinary phenomenon began when Albert was twenty-five years of age, and has spoken, on average, about once a week. The messages have varied from warning him of violent death to advising him to choose one particular make of motor car rather than another.

I know of only one other case like it, that of an American industrialist in the earlier part of this century. That case, however, although not without great dramatic moments, is infinitely less well documented, and all the witnesses to it are dead.

Albert at first received these messages with typical twentieth-century scepticism, imagining that his unconscious mind was giving him advice that his conscious mind was not eager to accept – that is, he gave the 'voice' a classically Freudian explanation. All this changed on 28 April 1960, when he was preparing to go on a combined holiday and business trip to North Africa. A few hours before the plane was due to leave, the voice said, 'Do not go to Morocco.' It seemed to be more than some mere fanciful quirk of his mind – he had the feeling of something independent from himself being at work. So he changed his plans.

On 1 May an earthquake and tidal wave destroyed the Moroccan city of Agadir, where he would have been staying. Considerably shaken, he vowed to listen to his voice's advice on all subjects, and also to keep a diary of its messages.

In 1961 he met a girl at a dance and became very attached to her, putting the voice to its ultimate test. He was on the point of proposing to the girl when it said, 'Do not marry her. She is ill.' As she appeared to be in the best of health, Albert was placed in a dreadful situation. If anything, the warning only served to intensify the love he felt for her. If she *was* sick, he would help her (he was already quite wealthy), and he asked her to be his wife. It was she who insisted that they both have medical examinations, and these were arranged with separate doctors.

He was given a clean bill of health, but she was found to have leukaemia in its earliest stages. Although he begged her to marry him, she declined, refusing to burden him with a wife who would sicken and die quite quickly. She left him, and a period of great depression followed.

Albert still listened to, and obeyed, the voice, but with a heavy heart. It told him of certain investments he should make, which made him richer, and it gave him good, but trivial, advice not worth reporting in this story. Almost exactly two years after his beloved girl had left him, he heard that she had died, and he fell into a deep melancholia. His work began to suffer, and he recalls that the dreadful period might have been the end of his business hopes. It was then that the voice, for the first and only time, spoke to him as good and trusted friend might: 'All life is immortal – only her body is dead – you will meet again if that is what you both want.' Albert reports that from that time his spirits returned, as he felt that his unseen guide was speaking the truth and not simply consoling him.

Some months after that a new junior partner was taken on at the firm, a woman only slightly younger than himself, called Elaine. Right from the start they seemed to detest each other cordially, he finding it difficult even to be civil to her, and she seeming to find him intolerable company. To Albert's total astonishment the voice told him that he would marry Elaine. Things got no better until the evening of the firm's annual visit to the theatre, followed by supper – a lavish affair for the senior staff. All started auspiciously enough: the play was most amusing, supper was a great success. As chance would have it, Elaine and he were among the last to leave. The remaining guests made their goodbyes and drove from the restaurant car-park. Their party had stayed late, and the place closed while they were talking. She bade him a civil enough goodnight and went to her car. His was parked at the far end and, as he drove back, he saw her still there, the car refusing to start. It was in the days before the proliferation of mini-cabs, and they were far enough out from the centre of London to make getting a black cab virtually an impossibility. He offered her a lift and she accepted. As it transpired, she lived a good way out in Surrey, so the journey was a long one. Both were a little mellowed by good food and wine, and as they progressed, they found that they had a good deal in common, both apologizing profusely for their earlier aloofness. Six months later they were married. The voice had scored another notable triumph.

Perhaps the voice's most important contribution, other than saving his life, was to recommend the purchase of some shares in Australia, in an obscure mine that was later to become world-famous as Poseidon, the great nickel bubble. As readers may remember, those shares rose astronomically in value, only to plunge as quickly as they had risen. Those who bought cheap and sold dear made one of the most successful *coups* in modern financial history. The voice gave the same kind of advice in the late seventies, when silver also rose sharply.

Albert has not greedily used the wealth generated by the mysterious voice, although it has never made any suggestions as to the way he should use the proceeds of the information. Many charities have cause, albeit unknowingly, to be most grateful to this uncanny adviser.

The mystery of Albert Tanner's helpmate is unfathomable in the light of current knowledge. It knows the future, but it cares little about the quality of its information; it will supply advice of tremendous significance or comparative banality with equal aplomb. Why it has picked on Albert cannot be imagined – he is a nice enough chap but the first to see himself as possessing no special spirituality, certainly nothing to make him an effective possessor of a Fortunatus's purse. He is simply another example of the inexplicable things that happen to people in this world.

Naturally, Albert has again and again asked to know the identity of his unseen friend. He never receives an answer. It speaks in what Albert describes as 'a normal, modern voice'. He has likewise asked for advice he wanted, rather than just accepted what he was given. No response has ever been forthcoming. When the voice has spoken while he is in the company of others, no one else has ever seemed to hear it. He is intrigued to know whether it speaks to him while he is asleep, but there seems no way of finding this out.

The Ghost who Hanged a Murderer

Detective Chief Superintendent Malcolm Davies has retired from the West Country force he served with for over forty years, but his mind is still the razor-sharp one that made him one of the most feared CID officers in Britain.

Of all the cases he has had to deal with, the one that came to be dubbed 'the Riddle of the Handless Corpse' by some of the more sensational newspapers is the one he remembers best. This is due partly to the horrific nature of the crime itself but mainly to the bizarre circumstances surrounding the way it was cleared up. None of the facts contained in this statement was ever revealed in court, and this is the first time he has spoken of the strange events that led to the arrest and execution of a brutal killer.

Older readers may remember the case, as it caused quite a stir in its time. Briefly, the facts are these: a young man out walking his dog discovered the corpse of a middle-aged woman in a field close to his home; upon investigation it transpired that she had been strangled, and Malcolm Davies, then a chief inspector, was given the job of identifying the woman and bringing the culprit to justice.

It became immediately apparent that the killing was not a local one. Forensic evidence quickly established that the woman had been murdered elsewhere and the body dumped well away from the scene of the crime. A gruesome addition to the murder, and one which caught the public's imagination, was that the murderer had severed both hands from the body. Davies immediately concluded that this had been done to prevent fingerprints being taken from the dead woman. If this was correct, it must have been because the woman had a criminal record and thus police-recorded fingerprints. Accordingly, he had a number of photographs taken of the corpse, and a local artist, who had helped the police before, was called on to produce a picture of what the woman would have looked like when alive. This was then circulated to every police station in the country. Results were not long in coming, and she was identified as Louise Trafford, who had quite a formidable police record in London and other large cities. She had been a prostitute in her younger days and had recently been suspected of being a fence and a supplier of weapons for armed robberies. Her flat was searched and found to have been looted of everything of any value; there were also signs of a violent struggle, and a copious amount of blood was found on the kitchen floor, where it was presumed the amputation of the hands had taken place.

The area in which Louise Trafford had lived is not one where the police can expect much help, although murder of one of your own is the worst breach of the code that criminals live by. The investigation was thorough and painstaking but yielded nothing, and Davies realized that he would have to give up the case, his skills being needed back home to counter one of those periodic and inexplicable outbreaks of crime. Leaving the matter in the competent hands of the Metropolitan Police, he reluctantly returned to the more mundane world of house-breaking, livestock-theft and fraud.

Some weeks passed and the case of the handless woman was pushed into the background. One morning, however, Davies received a strange letter. It was from a lady who claimed that she might have information concerning the murder, adding that she was a Spiritualist. It is only in books that the police disregard such people without exploring what they have to say. Since the police were first assisted by a psychic in the Jack the Ripper murders, many remarkable things have been achieved by these people, especially in the unearthing of missing evidence and persons. The Dutch seem to be particularly gifted in this, and most Western law-enforcement agencies, including Scotland Yard, the Sûreté and the FBI, have had cause to use such unorthodox methods, often with spectacular success.

Taking his sergeant and a tape-recorder with him, Davies kept the evening appointment with the clairvoyant. A maid showed them into a truly splendid library, in which a table and three chairs had been placed for the seance. The books themselves were a revelation – there were a number on psychic matters, but these were greatly outnumbered by mathematical works of considerable scholarship. It was while Davies was examining one that the medium entered. She was a tall and distinguished woman in her early fifties, quite unlike the stereotype the police officers had expected. In the conversation that followed it turned out that she had been a university lecturer and had a degree in physics. The classic myth of a clairvoyant being a silly old woman who stares into the bottoms of teacups was further shattered when they discovered that she was an authority on transfinite numbers, a new mathematical concept of which Davies' son, a second-year maths student, spoke with awe.

They sat at the table, and their hostess turned down the lights just enough to avoid any glare, leaving the room quite bright enough for Davies to make fine adjustments to his tape-recorder.

The medium explained that for the past three weeks, during seances involving other people, the presence of a woman had been detected, seemingly desperate to make contact. Nothing specific had been said, but she had 'felt' that the spirit was that of the woman left in the field. She went on to add that she was what was called a 'direct-voice' medium, which meant that the spirits spoke using her vocal cords, although sometimes they made themselves heard by other means. At that she began to try to make contact with the dead woman. The minutes ticked by and the atmosphere was electric. Both police officers felt tense and excited as the medium's breathing slowed and her face relaxed. Without any warning there came a sudden banging from what appeared to be the centre of the table: a rhythmic tattoo, like morse. This continued for two or three minutes, then stopped. Davies reports that he was completely shaken by this awesome display of power and quite bewildered as to its meaning. The medium had not returned to normality and, in accordance with instructions, they remained perfectly still and silent. Suddenly the noise began again, even more insistent than before. When it had finished, the medium came slowly out of her trance and asked if the results had been helpful. Still a little shaky, Davies played back the recordings of the mysterious tappings. She frowned in puzzlement and could offer no suggestion other than the fairly obvious one that it was some sort of prearranged code to which they would need the key. They talked for some time, and the policemen learnt a lot about the possibilities there were for greater cooperation between responsible Spiritualists and the authorities.

Davies was convinced that he had in his possession a

vital clue, and he played the recording over and over again in the hope of something appearing in it, but in vain.

About a week later, leafing through the dossier the Met had sent down on the murdered woman, his eye fell on an item he had not paid any attention to before. The victim had spent a year in Holloway women's prison some years before, for malicious wounding. Greatly excited, he put through a priority call to the governor. Within minutes he had the name and last known address of Louise Trafford's cell-mate, a woman serving five years for manslaughter. She was extremely anxious to do anything she could to help track down the killer of her friend. That evening, in the company of a woman police officer, Davies interviewed her in her Birmingham flat.

As soon as the rappings were played, she started, then listened intently. She stopped him after only a few moments of the second part of the tape, explaining that it was a repeat of the first. It was, she said, a code of Louise's own invention for keeping in touch with other prisoners, as she had been what is known as a 'tobacco baron', a person who sells tobacco to other convicts for money or favours. As her deputy, the woman he was interviewing was as familiar with the code as Louise herself, and it was rapidly translated. To Davies' utter astonishment, the message named the killer, listed the property stolen from the flat and revealed that the hands had been buried under a compost heap in the murderer's garden.

Officers of the West Midlands Police promptly questioned a man and, faced with the stolen goods and the decomposing hands, he made a full confession. Three months later he went to the gallows, oblivious of the incredible meaning behind the formal words given by Chief Inspector Davies in his evidence – 'acting on information received'.

In Conclusion

The commonest place to see psychic happenings is at a seance. This doesn't require any special effort on your part, for the local Spiritualist church will always provide genuine seekers after truth with the opportunity to participate in these strange events. They won't require you to accept any of their beliefs, only to go with an open mind. Much rubbish is talked about Spiritualists and Spiritualism. On the whole they are the most likeable of religious people, demanding nothing more than that you should look at their evidence and come to a fair conclusion. They don't want your money or your commitment, just a fair hearing. If you don't want to give them a fair hearing, don't go to their meetings; they will certainly not come round to your door begging for it.

As I have said before, I am not a Spiritualist, but I have more time for them than any other group I can think of. Of course, there will be the odd crank or fraud, but the fundamental movement is based on common sense and the rejection of a set creed. Go along to an ordinary meeting at your local Spiritualist church and judge for yourself. There are no robes, no candles, no ritual and, above all, no set of beliefs you must subscribe to. It's worth the trip, if only for the friendly atmosphere.

A seance is a group of people who believe that if they unite their spiritual powers they can communicate with people who have died – and sometimes with more powerful spirits who correspond more or less to angels (that is to say, they have not been living people once but are forces for good). Healing and other activities are involved, but the basic scenario is a group of people gathered together to gain and give solace, and get information from the world beyond this life. If you doubt, it doesn't matter; the important thing is to muster the psychic energy needed to make contact.

When the seance has started, often in a dimmed but by no means darkened room, the person who is leading the group, the medium, will ask if there is anyone waiting to come through and speak. Then the spirits either do or they don't, and if they do, they can do it in various ways. Often they speak through the person running the seance, or they may choose to move a glass towards letters placed around a table. In 'The Ghost who Hanged a Murderer', the spirit made herself clear without going via the medium, and this is the most unusual and spectacular of sittings.

Generally, the messages will be of a homely nature, each seemingly fitting a particular person in the group. I am not sure if the spirits of long-dead people come to ordinary surburban houses simply by being asked, but I can think of no *good* reason why they shouldn't, and I have heard enough to make me wonder very seriously.

This is not the world of 'The Flower Girl' or 'Doctor in the House' – they are special visitations, and we should not expect them at an ordinary seance. If evidence like that came through on an everyday basis, the whole world would have been converted long ago.

Let me give some examples of the sort of thing that happens.

Strangers are at the seance, and the medium says, 'John asks me to ask you to tell Sheila that he is OK, and that she is not to worry any more about the geranium. Does that mean anything to you?' It is so moving to see these people's faces light up, their heads nodding vigorously. Lucky guesses don't come into it – you try to pick two names and a circumstance that pleases two strangers and you'll find it impossible. That may be telepathy (if that phenomenon actually exists in the form it is supposed to), but in many cases it can't be, because the events referred to don't come to light until later, so that they cannot be known at the time of the seance. For instance, the medium may say, 'Mary is most anxious about a ticket that you should have. Does that mean anything?' It doesn't, but later a pawn ticket is found by chance which has significance for the family. Such instances rule out telepathy and indicate the psychic explanation.

I have made a point of talking to people after the meeting, and it really is astonishing. For example, a couple did have a son called John whose wife, Sheila, has always regretted letting a geranium he gave her die. In any given case, or even group of cases, you can postulate some reason for it other than the Spiritualist answer, but when it happens consistently, you have to ask yourself whether the disclaimers aren't more improbable than the evidence.

At one seance I organized with friends (a practice I warn against), the glass flew around the ouija board at great speed (it has been shown scientifically many times that one person, or even two people, cannot manipulate such a fast-moving object). It spelt out strange pieces of information, all disjointed. We looked at the transcript afterwards and, quite discernibly written, time after time, was the maiden name of one of the women present, and a fairly unusual one at that. On paper, that doesn't sound like any great evidence, especially after reading the amazing occurrences in this book, but it *is* odd how these things keep cropping up. I'm not hoodwinked easily – my professional career couldn't survive it, and I have recognized honest mistakes and deliberate deception in Spiritualism, but the overall impression is one of an underlying truth. This prompted me to go out and find out in greater depth exactly what had happened to people at the topmost level of the psychic experience, and this book is the result.

The seance, and the whole Spiritualist movement, is not about thrill-seeking, although there will be exciting times, but about a greater communion with whatever is *really* going on with life, and what may follow life. It is a step forward from the earlier religious concepts in one sense, and a going back to basics in another. It really isn't any good my saying these things: you must give it a try and see if it suits your temperament; the fact that you are reading this book shows that you have decided you want to look further than the mundane – not to reject the world of science and technology, Heaven forbid, but to examine all the possibilities there are for exploration of a world infinitely more complex than even our parents thought possible. It seems to me that science, far from negating the idea of psychic forces, has (did scientists but realize it) made them seem all the more plausible. It is not for any group to reject out of hand a large body of evidence just because a few cranks and frauds have appeared. It is for us to go forward with the common goal of discovering the truth, be it marvellous or depressing. In bringing to light just some of the experiences people have had, so that we can talk about them and test them, I hope I have contributed to a debate that I'm sure will lead us to a conclusion far sooner than any of us imagines.